The DHB Method: Leading with Decency

Introduction

In today's fast-paced corporate world, where the bottom line often overshadows human connection, there emerges a beacon of hope: The DHB Method. At its core, this method is a simple yet profound reminder that sometimes, the key to a thriving workplace isn't found in complex strategies or high-tech solutions. Instead, it lies in the age-old principle of being a "Decent Human Being."

Imagine a workplace where employees wake up excited to start their day, where creativity flows as freely as coffee, and where the sound of genuine laughter isn't a rarity but a daily occurrence. This isn't a utopian dream but a tangible reality for organizations that embrace the DHB Method.

But what does it mean to be a "Decent Human Being" in the context of management? Is it about being nice all the time? Or is it about avoiding conflicts? As we'll explore in the coming chapters, it's much more than that. It's about leading with empathy, integrity, and respect. It's about understanding that every decision, no matter how small, has a human impact. And most importantly, it's about recognizing that the most valuable asset in any organization isn't its products, services, or technologies, but its people.

In this book, we'll delve deep into the principles of the DHB Method, drawing from real-life success stories, scientific research, and practical insights. We'll also sprinkle in some humor because, let's face it, who doesn't need a good chuckle now and then? Especially when discussing topics as serious as management and leadership.

So, whether you're a seasoned CEO, an aspiring manager, or someone who just wants to bring a positive change to their workplace, this book is for you. Let's embark on this journey together and discover the transformative power of simply being a Decent Human Being.

Chapter 1: Understanding the DHB Method

In the vast sea of management theories, methodologies, and buzzwords, the DHB Method stands out, not because of its complexity, but because of its simplicity. At its heart, the DHB Method is a call to return to the basics of human interaction, to lead with authenticity, and to recognize the inherent value in every individual. In this chapter, we'll unpack the essence of the DHB Method and explore how it contrasts with traditional management styles.

Defining the DHB Method

The DHB Method, where DHB stands for "Decent Human Being," is a management approach rooted in the principles of empathy, respect, integrity, and kindness. It's not about being the smartest person in the room or having the most impressive resume. Instead, it's about:

1. **Seeing and valuing people**: Recognizing that every team member, regardless of their role or seniority, brings unique value to the table. "Seeing and valuing people" is a foundational principle that underscores the importance of recognizing the inherent worth and unique

contributions of every individual within an organization. In the intricate dynamics of a workplace, it's easy for individuals, especially those in non-leadership roles, to feel overshadowed or undervalued. However, true leadership recognizes that every team member, irrespective of their designated role or level of seniority, brings a distinct blend of experiences, skills, perspectives, and insights to the collective effort. This principle urges leaders to move beyond hierarchical perceptions and genuinely appreciate the diverse tapestry of talents and backgrounds that each person contributes. By doing so, leaders not only foster a culture of respect and inclusivity but also harness the full potential of their teams, ensuring that every voice is heard and every contribution is acknowledged.

2. **Leading with empathy**: Understanding and resonating with the emotions and perspectives of others.

   "Leading with empathy" is a transformative approach to leadership that goes beyond the mere execution of tasks and delves into the realm of human connection. It's about leaders immersing themselves in the emotional and cognitive worlds of their team members, striving to understand their feelings, motivations, challenges, and aspirations. This empathetic understanding allows leaders to resonate with the diverse perspectives within their teams, fostering a sense of trust and open communication. When leaders lead with empathy, they create an environment where individuals feel genuinely understood and valued, not just for their professional contributions but for their holistic selves. Such an environment not only enhances team cohesion and morale but also drives individuals to invest more deeply in their roles, knowing that their leader truly cares about their well-being and growth.

3. **Acting with integrity**: Being honest, transparent, and consistent in all actions and decisions.

   "Acting with integrity" is a principle that stands as the bedrock of trustworthy leadership. It emphasizes the importance of leaders being unwaveringly honest, transparent, and consistent in their actions and decisions. In the complex landscape of organizational dynamics, where multiple interests often intersect, it's easy for leaders to be swayed by short-term gains or external pressures. However, leading with integrity means making choices that align with core values, even when they might not be the easiest or most popular. It's about being transparent in intentions and actions, ensuring that team members are never left in the dark about decisions that affect them. Moreover, consistency in behavior and decision-making reinforces trust, as team members come to believe in a leader's reliability. In essence, when leaders act with unwavering integrity, they build a foundation of trust and respect, creating an environment where team members feel secure, valued, and motivated to give their best.

4. **Promoting a culture of respect**: Ensuring that every individual feels valued, heard, and respected.

   "Promoting a culture of respect" is a pivotal aspect of leadership that goes beyond mere professional courtesy and delves into the very fabric of organizational culture. It's the commitment of leaders to create an environment where every individual, irrespective of their role, background, or beliefs, is treated with genuine regard and consideration. This means not just acknowledging contributions but actively ensuring that every voice is given a platform and every concern is addressed. In such a culture, respect isn't just a top-down directive; it's a mutual understanding that permeates every interaction, meeting, and decision. When leaders prioritize and champion this culture, they send a powerful message about the organization's values. It fosters a sense of belonging and security among team members, knowing that they are in an environment where their dignity is upheld, their contributions are valued, and their perspectives are actively sought. In the long run, a culture steeped in respect not only enhances team cohesion and morale but also drives innovation and collaboration, as individuals feel empowered to share ideas and feedback without fear of retribution or dismissal.

Contrasting with Traditional Management Styles
Traditional management often emphasizes hierarchy, control, and results, sometimes at the expense of human connection. While achieving targets and maintaining order are essential, the DHB Method argues that these can be achieved more effectively when leaders prioritize human values. Here's a brief comparison:

- **Command and Control vs. Collaborative Leadership**:
  The traditional "Command and Control" style of leadership, prevalent in many organizations, operates on a top-down approach. In this model, decisions are primarily made by those at the highest echelons of the organizational hierarchy, and the directives then cascade down to be implemented by those at the lower rungs. While this might ensure streamlined decision-making, it often stifles creativity, discourages open communication, and can lead to a disconnect between leadership and the broader workforce. In contrast, the DHB Method champions the ethos of collaborative leadership. This approach recognizes the value of diverse perspectives and actively seeks input from

individuals across all levels of the organization. By promoting a culture where ideas and feedback are not just welcomed but actively encouraged, collaborative leadership fosters a sense of ownership and engagement among team members. It bridges the gap between senior leadership and frontline employees, ensuring that decisions are more holistic, well-informed, and resonate with the collective wisdom of the entire team. In essence, while the command and control model prioritizes authority, the DHB Method's collaborative leadership emphasizes partnership, mutual respect, and shared purpose.

- **Results at Any Cost vs. Sustainable Success**: Traditional leadership models often operate under a "results at any cost" mentality, placing paramount importance on achieving targets, often at the expense of the team's well-being. This approach might yield short-term gains, but it risks long-term sustainability as it can lead to burnout, high turnover, and diminished team morale. On the other hand, the DHB approach introduces a paradigm shift towards "sustainable success." Rather than viewing results and team well-being as mutually exclusive, the DHB method intertwines them, recognizing that true success isn't just about hitting numbers but ensuring that it's achieved in a manner that upholds the well-being and growth of every team member. This perspective acknowledges that a motivated, healthy, and engaged team is more likely to produce consistent, high-quality results over time. In the DHB framework, leaders are encouraged to balance ambition with empathy, drive with understanding, ensuring that the journey to success is as valued as the destination itself.

- **Rigid Structures vs. Flexibility**: Traditional management styles often lean heavily on rigid structures, where strict protocols, predefined processes, and a stringent adherence to rules dominate the organizational landscape. While this can bring about a sense of order and predictability, it often stifles creativity, innovation, and the ability to adapt to changing circumstances. Such rigidity can also be impersonal, failing to account for the unique needs, strengths, and challenges of individual team members. In stark contrast, the DHB

Method champions the principle of flexibility. It recognizes that in the dynamic world of modern business, adaptability is key. Moreover, it understands that every team member is a unique individual, with distinct aspirations, challenges, and ways of working. By valuing flexibility, the DHB approach allows for tailored solutions, both in terms of project execution and in addressing the diverse needs of the team. This not only fosters a more inclusive and responsive work environment but also empowers team members to bring their best selves to work, knowing that the organization values their individuality and is willing to adapt for their success and well-being.

The Evolution of the DHB Method

While the principles of decency, empathy, and respect are timeless, their application in the workplace has evolved over time. The rise of remote work, the emphasis on mental health, and the global call for inclusivity have all reinforced the need for a management style that prioritizes human connection. In the past, being a "Decent Human Being" in management might have been seen as a weakness or a lack of ambition. Today, it's recognized as one of the most potent tools for fostering innovation, loyalty, and productivity.

In Conclusion

The DHB Method isn't a trend or a fleeting management fad. It's a call to action, a reminder that in the midst of spreadsheets, meetings, and targets, the human element remains the most crucial factor. As we delve deeper into the subsequent chapters, we'll explore how to practically implement the DHB Method in various aspects of leadership and management, ensuring that decency becomes the cornerstone of your leadership journey.

Chapter 2: The Pillars of Decency

In the realm of management, the term "decency" might seem abstract or even subjective. However, when we talk about the DHB Method, decency is anchored in four foundational pillars: Empathy, Respect, Integrity, and Kindness. These pillars not only define what it means to be a "Decent Human Being" in leadership but also provide a roadmap for managers to cultivate a positive and productive work environment. Let's delve into each of these pillars and understand their significance.

1. Empathy: Walking in Their Shoes

Empathy is the ability to understand and share the feelings of another. In a managerial context, it means:

- **Understanding Team Dynamics**: Recognizing the challenges, pressures, and aspirations of team members.

  Understanding team dynamics is a nuanced aspect of leadership that delves deeper than just recognizing the roles and responsibilities of team members. It's about truly grasping the intricate web of relationships, motivations, challenges, and aspirations that shape the collective psyche of a team. Leaders who prioritize this understanding recognize that beyond the professional facades, every team member grapples with their own set of pressures, both from within the workplace and outside of it. They might be striving to meet personal goals, dealing with external stresses, or navigating the complexities of interpersonal relationships within the team. By taking the time to understand these dynamics, leaders can create an environment where challenges are addressed with empathy, pressures are mitigated through support, and aspirations are nurtured through opportunities and mentorship. This holistic approach not only enhances the well-being and productivity of individual team members but also strengthens the cohesiveness and resilience of the team as a whole, ensuring that they can navigate both triumphs and trials with solidarity and grace.

- **Active Listening**: Paying full attention to what others are saying, understanding the complete message, and responding thoughtfully. Active listening is a profound communication skill that transcends mere hearing and delves into the realm of deep understanding and genuine engagement. It's not just about catching the words spoken but truly grasping the emotions, intentions, and nuances behind them. When leaders practice active listening, they're not just waiting for their turn to speak; they're fully immersed in the conversation, paying undivided attention to the speaker. This attentive stance allows them to comprehend the complete message, both the overt content and the subtle undertones. But active listening doesn't stop at understanding; it extends to responding thoughtfully, ensuring that the speaker feels truly heard and valued. Such interactions foster trust, open communication, and mutual respect. In the context of leadership, active listening becomes even more pivotal. It signals to team members that their perspectives, concerns, and ideas are not just acknowledged but deeply valued, creating an environment where open dialogue and collaboration thrive.

- **Emotional Resonance**: Feeling with people, not just for them. This involves sharing in their joys, concerns, and challenges.

  Emotional resonance is a profound level of

emotional connection that goes beyond mere sympathy or understanding. It's about truly immersing oneself in the emotional experiences of others, feeling alongside them rather than observing from a distance. When leaders embody emotional resonance, they don't just acknowledge the emotions of their team members; they deeply share in them. This means celebrating the joys and successes of team members as if they were their own, genuinely feeling concern when challenges arise, and standing shoulder to shoulder during tough times. Such a connection creates a bond that is both powerful and nurturing. In the context of leadership, emotional resonance fosters a sense of unity and mutual trust. Team members feel seen, understood, and deeply valued, knowing that their leader is emotionally invested in their well-being and success. This not only enhances team cohesion and morale but also creates a supportive environment where individuals feel safe to express themselves, share their aspirations, and voice their concerns, knowing they will be met with genuine empathy and understanding.

Benefits:

- Builds trust and rapport.

- Facilitates open communication.

- Enhances team cohesion and collaboration.

2. Respect: Valuing Every Individual

Respect is about treating everyone with dignity, regardless of their role, background, or beliefs. It involves:

- **Acknowledging Contributions**: Recognizing and appreciating the efforts of every team member.

  Acknowledging contributions is a fundamental aspect of leadership that extends beyond mere recognition of tasks completed. It's about genuinely valuing the time, effort, creativity, and dedication that every team member pours into their work. When leaders prioritize acknowledging contributions, they send a powerful message to their team: every effort, no matter how big or small, is noticed and appreciated. This act of recognition and appreciation does more than just boost morale; it fosters a sense of belonging and purpose among team members. They feel that their work has meaning, that they are integral to the organization's success, and that their contributions are making a tangible difference. In the grand tapestry of organizational dynamics, where goals and targets often take center stage, taking the time to acknowledge and appreciate individual contributions ensures that the human element remains at the forefront. It reinforces the idea that behind every achievement, there's a team of dedicated individuals whose efforts and commitment made it all possible. By consistently acknowledging these contributions, leaders cultivate an environment of mutual respect, motivation, and a shared sense of accomplishment.

- **Avoiding Favoritism**: Ensuring that decisions are made fairly, without biases.
  Avoiding favoritism is a crucial tenet of ethical leadership, emphasizing the importance of fairness and impartiality in decision-making. In the intricate dynamics of a workplace, where personal relationships and affinities can naturally develop, it's essential for leaders to remain vigilant against allowing these

connections to influence professional decisions. Favoritism, whether perceived or real, can erode trust, breed resentment, and disrupt the harmony of a team. When leaders prioritize avoiding favoritism, they're sending a clear message to their team: every individual is valued based on their merit, contributions, and capabilities, rather than personal affiliations or biases. This commitment to fairness ensures that opportunities, rewards, and recognitions are distributed based on objective criteria, fostering a sense of justice and equity within the team. Moreover, by consistently making decisions without biases, leaders not only uphold the integrity of their position but also cultivate a culture where team members feel secure, knowing that their efforts will be recognized and rewarded based solely on their performance and potential.

- **Promoting Inclusivity**: Creating an environment where everyone feels they belong and can voice their opinions without fear. Promoting inclusivity is more than just a leadership strategy; it's a commitment to fostering a workplace culture that celebrates

diversity in all its forms and ensures every
individual feels valued and heard. In an
inclusive environment, differences—whether in
terms of background, beliefs, experiences, or
perspectives—are not just tolerated but actively
embraced as assets that enrich the collective
wisdom of the team. Leaders who prioritize
inclusivity recognize that true innovation and
growth stem from a mosaic of diverse insights
and ideas. But inclusivity goes beyond just
recognizing diversity; it's about creating a safe
space where every team member feels they
truly belong, irrespective of their differences.
It's an environment where voicing opinions,
sharing unique perspectives, or raising
concerns is encouraged, and where every
contribution is met with respect and
consideration. By actively promoting inclusivity,
leaders not only enhance the creativity and
dynamism of their teams but also build a
foundation of trust, mutual respect, and shared
purpose, ensuring that every individual feels
integral to the organization's journey and
success.

Benefits:

- Boosts morale and self-worth.

- Reduces conflicts and grievances.

- Encourages diversity of thought and innovation.

3. Integrity: Leading by Example

Integrity is about being honest, transparent, and consistent. It's the backbone of trust and credibility. For managers, this means:

- **Honest Communication**: Being upfront about challenges, changes, and expectations. Honest communication stands as a pillar of effective leadership, emphasizing the importance of transparency and forthrightness in all interactions. In the ever-evolving landscape of a workplace, where challenges arise, changes are inevitable, and expectations shift, it's imperative for leaders to maintain a clear channel of communication with their teams. Being upfront about challenges ensures that team members are not blindsided but are prepared and can proactively adapt to situations. Transparently discussing changes, whether they are organizational shifts or alterations in strategy, fosters trust and ensures that everyone is aligned with the evolving vision. Furthermore, clarity about expectations eliminates ambiguity, allowing team members to understand their roles and responsibilities better and work towards defined goals. Leaders who prioritize honest communication create an environment of mutual respect, where team members feel valued not just for their contributions but also for their right to be informed and involved. Such an approach not only bolsters team morale and cohesion but also reinforces the idea that every individual is a valued stakeholder in the organization's journey, deserving of transparency and trust.

- **Consistency in Actions**: Ensuring that actions align with words and promises.
  Consistency in actions is a hallmark of trustworthy leadership, underscoring the significance of aligning deeds with declarations. In the multifaceted world of leadership, where words hold power and promises set expectations, it's paramount for leaders to ensure that their actions mirror their commitments. When leaders consistently act in

harmony with their words, they build a foundation of reliability and credibility. Team members, in turn, develop a sense of security, knowing that they can take their leader's words at face value, confident in the knowledge that promises will be honored and commitments fulfilled. Conversely, a disconnect between words and actions can erode trust, breed skepticism, and diminish morale. Leaders who prioritize consistency in their actions not only fortify the trust and respect of their teams but also set a powerful example, fostering a culture where integrity, accountability, and authenticity are valued and practiced at all levels of the organization. In essence, consistency in actions reinforces the age-old adage that actions, indeed, speak louder than words, especially in the realm of leadership.

- **Owning Mistakes**: Taking responsibility for errors and working towards rectifying them. Owning mistakes is a testament to a leader's humility, accountability, and commitment to growth. In the intricate dance of leadership, where perfection is often sought but rarely achieved, the ability to acknowledge and take responsibility for errors stands out as a defining trait. When leaders own their mistakes, they send a clear message to their teams: that it's okay to be fallible, and what truly matters is the willingness to learn and grow from those missteps. Such an approach not only humanizes leaders, making them more relatable and approachable, but also fosters a culture of transparency and continuous improvement. By taking responsibility for errors, leaders also set a precedent of accountability, encouraging their teams to do the same. This creates an environment where mistakes are viewed not as failures but as opportunities for learning and betterment. Moreover, by actively working towards rectifying errors, leaders demonstrate resilience, determination, and a commitment to excellence. In essence, owning mistakes and addressing them head-on not only enhances a leader's credibility but also strengthens the trust, respect, and loyalty of their teams, paving the way for a more collaborative, understanding, and growth-oriented work environment.

Benefits:

- Builds trust and credibility.

- Encourages a culture of accountability.

- Enhances organizational reputation.

4. Kindness: Going the Extra Mile

Kindness in management isn't about being overly lenient or avoiding tough decisions. It's about:

- **Showing Genuine Concern**: Taking an interest in the well-being of team members, both professionally and personally. Showing genuine concern is an embodiment of leadership that transcends the confines of professional roles and delves into the realm of authentic human connection. Leaders who exhibit genuine concern recognize that their team members are not just cogs in a machine but multifaceted individuals with aspirations, challenges, and lives outside of work. By taking a sincere interest in the well-being of their team members, both in their professional endeavors and personal lives, leaders foster a deep sense of trust and loyalty. This genuine concern signals to team members that they are valued not just for their output or skills but as whole individuals. Such an approach creates a nurturing work environment where team members feel supported, understood, and appreciated. Moreover, by showing genuine concern, leaders cultivate a culture of empathy and compassion, where team members are more likely to support one another, collaborate effectively, and invest wholeheartedly in their roles. In the grand tapestry of leadership, showing genuine concern stands out as a thread that weaves together trust, loyalty, and a shared sense of purpose, creating a cohesive and motivated team.

- **Offering Support**: Providing resources, training, or even a listening ear when needed. Offering support is a tangible manifestation of a leader's commitment to the growth and well-being of their team members. In the dynamic landscape of the modern workplace, challenges are inevitable, and the path to success is often riddled with obstacles. Leaders who prioritize offering support recognize these challenges and proactively step in to provide the necessary resources, be it in the form of training, tools, or guidance. But support isn't just about tangible

resources; sometimes, it's about offering a
listening ear, understanding the concerns and
aspirations of team members, and providing
reassurance or advice. By being a consistent
pillar of support, leaders create an environment
where team members feel empowered to take
risks, innovate, and push boundaries, knowing
that they have a safety net of support to fall
back on. This not only boosts confidence and
morale but also fosters a culture of continuous
learning and resilience. In essence, offering
support is a testament to a leader's investment
in the success and well-being of their team,
ensuring that every individual has the tools,
resources, and emotional backing to thrive and
excel.

- **Celebrating Milestones**: Recognizing both
  professional achievements and personal
  milestones, like birthdays or anniversaries.
  Celebrating milestones is a testament to a
  leader's commitment to recognizing and valuing
  the multifaceted journeys of their team
  members. In the fast-paced world of work,
  where the focus is often on targets and
  deliverables, taking a moment to celebrate both

professional achievements and personal milestones stands out as a gesture of genuine appreciation. Recognizing professional accomplishments not only reinforces the value of hard work and dedication but also boosts morale, motivating team members to continue striving for excellence. On the other hand, acknowledging personal milestones, such as birthdays or anniversaries, adds a touch of warmth and personal connection, signaling to team members that they are seen and valued beyond their professional roles. By celebrating these moments, leaders foster a sense of belonging and camaraderie within the team, creating a work environment where individuals feel deeply connected, both to their work and to each other. In essence, celebrating milestones is a powerful tool in a leader's arsenal, weaving together the threads of professional dedication and personal connection to create a cohesive, motivated, and deeply engaged team.

Benefits:

- Boosts team morale and loyalty.

- Encourages a positive work environment.

- Enhances overall job satisfaction.

In Conclusion

The pillars of the DHB Method aren't just lofty ideals; they are actionable principles that every manager can incorporate into their leadership style. By embracing Empathy, Respect, Integrity, and Kindness, managers can transform their teams, fostering an environment of collaboration, innovation, and mutual respect. As we continue our journey through the DHB Method, we'll explore practical ways to embed these pillars into everyday management practices, ensuring that decency isn't just a concept but a lived reality.

Chapter 3: The Power of Active Listening

In the cacophony of the modern workplace—filled with meetings, emails, and constant notifications—one skill stands out as a beacon of effective leadership: Active Listening. While it might seem like a simple concept, true active listening goes beyond just hearing words. It's about understanding, processing, and responding to the underlying messages and emotions. In this chapter, we'll delve into the nuances of active listening and its pivotal role in the DHB Method.

Understanding Active Listening

At its core, active listening is a two-fold process:

1. **Absorbing Information**: This involves giving your undivided attention to the speaker, free from distractions, and truly hearing what they're saying.

   Absorbing information is a foundational aspect of effective communication, emphasizing the importance of truly immersing oneself in the act of listening. In our increasingly digital and fast-paced world, distractions are omnipresent, making genuine, undivided attention a rare commodity. When one commits to absorbing information, it's not just about passively hearing words; it's about actively engaging with the content, understanding the nuances, and grasping the underlying emotions and intentions of the speaker. This requires a conscious effort to set aside external distractions, be it digital devices or wandering thoughts, and hone in on the message being conveyed. By giving undivided attention, listeners not only gain a deeper understanding of the subject matter but also convey respect and value to the speaker. This act of genuine listening fosters trust, strengthens relationships, and ensures that crucial details and subtleties aren't overlooked. In essence, absorbing information is both an art and a skill, serving as a bridge to deeper understanding and more meaningful interactions.

2. **Reflecting and Responding**: This is about processing the information, understanding the emotions behind it, and providing a thoughtful response.
   Reflecting and responding is a nuanced continuation of the communication process, emphasizing the importance of internal

processing and thoughtful engagement. Once information is absorbed, true comprehension requires a moment of reflection, a pause to digest the content, and discern the emotions and motivations underlying the words. This reflective process ensures that responses aren't just reactive or superficial but are grounded in a deep understanding of the message conveyed. Moreover, by taking the time to understand the emotions behind the words, responders can tailor their feedback or comments in a way that resonates with the speaker's feelings and intentions. Providing a thoughtful response, in turn, fosters a sense of validation and respect, signaling to the speaker that their message has been genuinely understood and valued. In the intricate dance of human interaction, reflecting and responding serves as a pivotal step, bridging the gap between mere listening and meaningful dialogue, ensuring that conversations are not just exchanges of words but pathways to deeper connections and understanding.

Why Active Listening Matters in Management

- **Builds Trust**: Building trust is a cornerstone of effective leadership, and one of the most potent avenues to achieve this is through genuine listening. When team members feel that their voices are not just heard but deeply understood, it fosters a profound sense of validation and respect. This feeling transcends mere communication; it signals to the team that their perspectives, concerns, and insights are valued and considered in decision-making processes. Over time, this consistent act of attentive listening and understanding cultivates a foundation of trust. Team members become more confident in their leaders, believing that their best interests are at heart and that their contributions play a pivotal role in the organization's trajectory. In essence, the simple act of genuine listening becomes a powerful trust-building tool, weaving together the threads of respect, validation, and mutual understanding to create a cohesive and harmonious team environment.

- **Enhances Decision Making**: Enhancing decision-making is a critical facet of leadership, and the depth and breadth of understanding garnered from considering diverse perspectives play a pivotal role in this process. In the complex landscape of business and management, decisions are rarely black and white; they often exist in shades of gray, influenced by a myriad of factors and viewpoints. When managers actively seek and understand these varied perspectives, they equip themselves with a richer tapestry of information and insights. This holistic understanding allows them to weigh the pros and cons more effectively, anticipate potential challenges, and identify opportunities that might otherwise go unnoticed. Moreover, by valuing and incorporating the insights of team members from different backgrounds, roles, or experiences, managers not only foster inclusivity but also ensure that decisions are well-rounded and resilient. In essence, the act of understanding and integrating different perspectives doesn't just enhance the quality of decision-making; it also reinforces the idea that every voice matters, leading to more informed, collaborative, and effective outcomes.

- **Reduces Conflicts**: Reducing conflicts is
  essential for maintaining a harmonious and
  productive workplace environment, and active
  listening emerges as a key tool in this endeavor.
  At the heart of many workplace conflicts lies a
  simple yet profound issue: misunderstandings.
  Whether it's a misinterpretation of intentions, a
  miscommunication of expectations, or a lack of
  clarity in roles and responsibilities, these
  misunderstandings can quickly escalate into
  larger disputes if left unaddressed. Active
  listening serves as a proactive measure against
  such issues. By truly engaging with and
  understanding what another person is
  conveying, leaders and team members can
  identify potential points of contention early on
  and address them before they become
  problematic. Furthermore, when conflicts do
  arise, active listening becomes an invaluable
  tool for resolution. By giving each party the
  space to express their viewpoints and ensuring
  that they feel genuinely heard, it becomes
  easier to find common ground, clarify
  misconceptions, and collaboratively work
  towards a solution. In essence, active listening
  not only prevents the genesis of many conflicts

but also provides a pathway to navigate and resolve them, ensuring a more cohesive and understanding workplace.

Techniques to Enhance Active Listening Skills

1. **Minimize Distractions**: Whether it's turning off notifications or choosing a quiet space for conversations, ensure you're fully present. Minimizing distractions is a foundational step in the art of effective communication and active listening. In today's digital age, where a barrage of notifications, messages, and alerts constantly vie for our attention, being truly present in a conversation can be a challenge. However, the act of consciously turning off these distractions, be it silencing a smartphone or selecting a serene space for dialogue, signals a deep commitment to the conversation at hand. By doing so, individuals not only shield themselves from potential interruptions but also create an environment conducive to genuine engagement. Being fully present means immersing oneself in the conversation, absorbing every nuance, emotion, and detail. This level of attentiveness fosters deeper

understanding, builds trust, and conveys a sense of respect and value to the speaker. In essence, the act of minimizing distractions is more than just a logistical step; it's a conscious choice to prioritize human connection over digital intrusions, ensuring that conversations are meaningful, productive, and devoid of superficiality.

2. **Practice Patience**: Allow the speaker to finish their thoughts without interrupting. Resist the urge to formulate your response while they're still speaking.

   Practicing patience in communication is a testament to one's respect and genuine interest in understanding the speaker. In the ebb and flow of conversation, there's often a natural inclination to jump in, either to offer a perspective, ask a question, or even, at times, to finish the speaker's sentence. However, true comprehension requires restraint, allowing the speaker to fully articulate their thoughts without interruption. This patience ensures that the speaker feels valued, heard, and understood, fostering a deeper level of trust and openness in the conversation. Moreover, resisting the urge to formulate a response while the speaker is still talking is crucial. By doing so, one remains fully engaged in the present moment, absorbing the entirety of the message rather than just bits and pieces. This not only enhances understanding but also ensures that any subsequent response is thoughtful, relevant, and informed by the complete context of what was shared. In essence, practicing patience in communication is a deliberate act of respect and empathy, paving the way for richer, more meaningful interactions.

3. **Use Non-Verbal Cues**: Nodding, maintaining eye contact, and using open body language can make the speaker feel more at ease.
   Utilizing non-verbal cues is an integral component of effective communication, often speaking volumes even in the absence of words. These subtle gestures and expressions, such as nodding or maintaining eye contact, serve as silent affirmations, signaling to the speaker that they have the listener's undivided attention and their message is being received. Eye contact, in particular, fosters a sense of connection and sincerity, bridging the gap between speaker and

listener and creating an environment of trust. Meanwhile, open body language, like uncrossed arms or leaning slightly forward, conveys receptivity and genuine interest in the conversation. These non-verbal cues, when used appropriately, can significantly enhance the comfort level of the speaker, making them feel more at ease, valued, and encouraged to share openly. In the intricate dance of human interaction, non-verbal cues play a pivotal role, complementing verbal communication and ensuring that the essence of the message, along with its emotional undertones, is truly understood and acknowledged.

4. **Clarify and Paraphrase**: If something is unclear, ask for clarification. Occasionally, paraphrase what you've heard to ensure you've understood correctly.

   Clarifying and paraphrasing are essential tools in the arsenal of effective communication, acting as bridges between mere hearing and genuine understanding. In the course of a conversation, especially when complex ideas or emotions are being conveyed, there's always the potential for certain points to become ambiguous or misinterpreted. By actively seeking clarification when something is unclear, listeners demonstrate a genuine desire to fully grasp the speaker's message, ensuring that no crucial details are overlooked or misconstrued. This proactive approach not only enhances comprehension but also fosters trust, as the speaker feels valued and assured that their message is being taken seriously. Paraphrasing, on the other hand, is a reflective technique where the listener occasionally restates what they've heard, albeit in their own words. This serves a dual purpose: it confirms to the speaker that their message has been accurately received and provides an opportunity for any misinterpretations to be promptly addressed. Together, clarifying and paraphrasing act as safeguards, ensuring that conversations are not just exchanges of words but meaningful dialogues rooted in mutual understanding and respect.

5. **Offer Empathetic Responses**: Instead of immediately jumping to solutions, sometimes it's more valuable to acknowledge the speaker's feelings and emotions.

Offering empathetic responses is a nuanced approach to communication, emphasizing the importance of emotional validation over immediate problem-solving. In many conversations, especially those charged with emotion or personal significance, the speaker's primary need isn't necessarily a quick solution but rather a sense of being truly heard and understood. By responding with empathy, listeners acknowledge the emotions and feelings underlying the words, providing a space for the speaker to express themselves without judgment or haste. This form of response creates a safe environment where the speaker feels valued, respected, and supported. While solutions and advice have their place, jumping to them prematurely can sometimes make the speaker feel dismissed or oversimplified. By prioritizing empathetic responses, listeners ensure that the emotional depth of the conversation is honored, fostering deeper connections and trust. In essence, empathy in communication is a testament to the understanding that sometimes the journey of sharing and being heard is just as important, if not more so, than arriving at a destination or solution.

The Impact of Active Listening on Team Morale and Productivity

- **Boosted Morale**: When employees feel heard, they're more likely to feel valued and satisfied in their roles.

  The act of truly listening to employees and making them feel heard is a powerful gesture that resonates deeply within the fabric of workplace dynamics. When employees feel that their voices, concerns, and ideas are genuinely acknowledged, it creates a profound sense of validation. This validation extends beyond the immediate conversation; it signals to employees that they are integral components of the organization, not just in terms of their functional roles but also as individuals with unique perspectives and experiences. This feeling of being valued fosters a deeper sense of job satisfaction, as employees perceive their roles not merely as tasks to be completed but as meaningful contributions to the larger organizational narrative. Moreover, when employees feel heard, they are more likely to engage proactively, offer innovative solutions, and invest emotionally in their work, leading to enhanced productivity and commitment. In essence, the simple act of listening and making employees feel heard lays the groundwork for a more motivated, engaged, and satisfied workforce, reinforcing the idea that every voice matters and every contribution is significant.

- **Increased Productivity**: Clear communication stands as a linchpin in the intricate machinery of workplace dynamics, ensuring that tasks, goals, and visions are conveyed with precision and understanding. In any organization, the flow of information is constant, with directives, feedback, and ideas crisscrossing between various levels and departments. When this communication is clear and unambiguous, it drastically reduces the potential for misunderstandings or misinterpretations, which can often lead to errors, delays, or misaligned efforts. By ensuring that everyone is on the same page, clear communication streamlines work processes, allowing teams to function cohesively and move forward with a unified purpose. Furthermore, when employees have a clear understanding of their roles, expectations, and the broader organizational goals, they can execute their tasks with greater confidence and efficiency. In essence, clear communication acts as a lubricant for the organizational engine, minimizing friction, enhancing collaboration, and ensuring that the entire workforce marches in harmony towards shared objectives.

- **Enhanced Innovation**: Active listening, when practiced by managers and leaders, becomes a catalyst for fostering a vibrant culture of innovation and creativity within an organization. Team members, when they feel genuinely heard and understood, are more inclined to share their ideas, insights, and feedback without reservation. This open channel of communication creates a fertile ground for fresh perspectives and novel solutions to emerge. Managers who prioritize active listening are not just collecting feedback; they're signaling to their teams that every idea, regardless of its origin, holds potential value and merit. This validation encourages a mindset of continuous exploration and experimentation among team members, leading to a plethora of innovative solutions to challenges. Moreover, when creativity is met with genuine interest and consideration, it reinforces a culture where innovation is not just welcomed but celebrated. In essence, the act of active listening by managers becomes a powerful tool, transforming the workplace into a collaborative think-tank where boundaries are pushed, and new horizons are continually explored.

Common Barriers to Active Listening

1. **Preconceived Notions**: Entering a conversation laden with preconceived notions or strong biases can significantly impede the process of genuine understanding. Such biases act as filters, coloring the information received and often leading to misinterpretations or selective hearing. Instead of absorbing the message in its entirety, individuals with strong preconceived notions tend to cherry-pick information that aligns with their existing beliefs, while unconsciously dismissing or overlooking details that might challenge them. This not only hampers effective communication

but also stifles the possibility of growth and learning from diverse perspectives. For true active listening to occur, it's essential to approach conversations with an open mind, setting aside biases and being receptive to new or differing viewpoints.

2. **Multitasking**: In today's fast-paced world, the allure of multitasking is undeniable. However, attempting to juggle multiple tasks simultaneously can severely dilute one's focus, undermining the effectiveness of active listening. When individuals split their attention between listening and other activities, they often miss out on the nuances, emotions, and subtleties of the conversation. This fragmented attention can lead to misunderstandings, misinterpretations, and a general sense of disconnect between the speaker and the listener. For genuine communication to take place, it's imperative to be fully present in the moment, dedicating one's complete attention to the speaker and the message being conveyed.

3. **Emotional Reactions**: Emotions, especially intense ones, have the power to cloud judgment and skew perception. When individuals

experience strong emotional reactions during a conversation, it can act as a barrier to objective and effective listening. Emotions such as anger, defensiveness, or extreme excitement can narrow one's focus, leading to selective hearing or even complete shutdowns in communication. Instead of processing the information objectively, emotionally charged listeners might fixate on specific triggers, potentially missing the broader message or intent. To practice active listening, it's crucial to recognize and manage these emotional responses, ensuring that they don't overshadow the core of the conversation or hinder genuine understanding.

In Conclusion

Active listening is more than a skill; it's a commitment to understanding and valuing the perspectives of others. In the realm of the DHB Method, it's a cornerstone, ensuring that every interaction is rooted in empathy and respect. As we progress in our exploration of the DHB Method, we'll see how active listening intertwines with other principles, creating a tapestry of effective and compassionate leadership.

Chapter 4: The Role of Humor in Leadership

When one thinks of leadership qualities, humor might not be the first trait that comes to mind. However, in the context of the DHB Method, humor plays a pivotal role. It's not about cracking jokes every minute or turning the workplace into a comedy club. Instead, it's about leveraging the power of humor to build connections, alleviate stress, and foster a positive work environment. In this chapter, we'll explore the nuances of humor in leadership and its transformative impact.

The Science Behind Humor

Before diving into its application in leadership, let's understand the science of humor:

- **Endorphin Release** Laughter, often dubbed as nature's best medicine, has a profound physiological effect on the human body. One of its most notable impacts is the release of endorphins, which are neurotransmitters that act as the body's natural painkillers and mood elevators. When individuals laugh, there's a surge of these feel-good chemicals, leading to sensations of pleasure and euphoria. This not only elevates mood but also fosters a sense of camaraderie among those sharing the laughter. The communal aspect of laughter, combined with the endorphin release, creates an environment where individuals feel more connected, positive, and motivated, promoting an overall sense of well-being and cohesion.

- **Stress Reduction**: In the face of adversity or challenging situations, laughter emerges as a potent antidote to stress. When individuals laugh, there's a marked reduction in the production of stress hormones like cortisol. This physiological response acts as a natural buffer against the negative impacts of stress, helping individuals navigate challenges with greater resilience and equanimity. Moreover, laughter's ability to counteract stress extends beyond the immediate moment; its effects can linger, providing a sustained sense of relief and relaxation. In essence, laughter serves as a natural stress-reliever, helping individuals cope more effectively with challenges and maintain a balanced and positive outlook even in demanding situations.

- **Enhanced Creativity**: Beyond its physiological benefits, laughter plays a pivotal role in stimulating cognitive functions. A light-hearted and jovial environment acts as a catalyst for the brain, sparking creativity and encouraging divergent thinking. When individuals are in a setting where humor is valued and laughter is frequent, they often feel more liberated to think outside the box, explore unconventional solutions, and approach problems from unique angles. This heightened state of creativity is not just about generating novel ideas but also about fostering a culture where innovation is celebrated, risks are embraced, and the boundaries of conventional thinking are continually expanded. In short, laughter paves the way for a more dynamic, creative, and innovative mindset.

Incorporating Humor Without Crossing Boundaries

Humor is subjective, and what's funny to one person might be offensive to another. Here's how leaders can incorporate humor effectively:

1. **Know Your Audience**: For humor to be effective and appreciated, it's crucial for leaders to have a deep understanding of their audience. This involves recognizing the diverse cultural, social, and individual backgrounds of team members. Every individual comes with a unique set of experiences, values, and sensitivities, and what might be humorous to one person could be deeply unsettling or offensive to another. By taking the time to understand these nuances and being attuned to the team's dynamics, leaders can tailor their humor in a way that resonates positively, fostering a sense of camaraderie and inclusivity. In essence, knowing your audience is about striking a balance, ensuring that humor acts as a unifying force rather than a divisive one.

2. **Avoid Sensitive Topics**: While humor can be a powerful tool for engagement and connection, it's essential to navigate it with caution, especially when it comes to potentially sensitive topics. Leaders should be wary of humor that touches upon areas like race, gender, religion, or deeply personal issues. Such topics, given their inherent sensitivities, can easily lead to

misunderstandings or even cause unintended
harm. By steering clear of these areas, leaders
ensure that their attempts at humor uplift and
entertain without alienating or offending any
team members. It's always better to err on the
side of caution and prioritize the well-being and
comfort of the team over a fleeting moment of
laughter.

3. **Self-deprecating Humor**: One of the safest
   and most endearing forms of humor a leader
   can employ is self-deprecation. Making light-
   hearted jokes or playful remarks about oneself
   can humanize leaders, making them more
   relatable and approachable to their teams. This
   form of humor showcases vulnerability and
   humility, signaling to team members that it's
   okay to be imperfect and have a laugh about it.
   Moreover, by directing the humor at oneself,
   leaders minimize the risk of inadvertently
   offending others. However, it's essential to
   strike a balance; while occasional self-
   deprecating humor can be endearing, overdoing
   it might undermine a leader's credibility or
   authority.

4. **Encourage Light-hearted Moments**: Beyond personal attempts at humor, leaders can foster a jovial work environment by creating opportunities for team members to share their own funny anecdotes or experiences. Whether it's setting aside a few minutes during meetings for light-hearted banter or organizing team-building activities with a humorous twist, these moments can act as valuable breaks from the daily grind. They not only infuse a sense of fun into the workplace but also strengthen bonds among team members. By encouraging such moments, leaders cultivate a culture where laughter and joy are integral, promoting overall well-being and job satisfaction.

Case Studies: Successful Leaders Who Lead with Humor

Throughout history, many successful leaders have effectively used humor:

- **Richard Branson**: The iconic founder of the Virgin Group, has long been celebrated not just for his entrepreneurial prowess but also for his distinctive, playful approach to business. Unlike many traditional business magnates who

maintain a strictly formal demeanor, Branson
has consistently infused a sense of fun and
adventure into his professional endeavors. This
is evident in the numerous stunts, pranks, and
unconventional promotional activities he's
undertaken over the years. Whether it's
attempting to circumnavigate the globe in a hot
air balloon, dressing up in flamboyant costumes,
or playfully challenging competitors, Branson's
antics have often captured headlines and the
public's imagination. But beyond mere publicity
stunts, these actions reflect Branson's core
belief in not taking oneself too seriously and
ensuring that business, while being about
profits and growth, should also be fun and
invigorating. His unique style has not only set
him apart in the corporate world but has also
played a role in shaping the vibrant,
unconventional ethos of the Virgin brand.

- **Mary Barra**: The trailblazing CEO of General
  Motors stands as a testament to the power of
  combining strong leadership with a touch of
  levity. While she's widely recognized for her
  decisive and forward-thinking leadership style,
  steering one of the world's largest automobile

companies through transformative times, it's her adept use of humor that adds a unique dimension to her leadership persona. In her speeches, presentations, and day-to-day interactions, Barra often weaves in humorous anecdotes, light-hearted remarks, or witty observations. This approach does more than just entertain; it humanizes her, making her more relatable to employees across all levels of the organization. By incorporating humor, she bridges the gap that often exists between top-tier executives and the broader workforce, fostering a sense of camaraderie and mutual respect. In essence, Barra's use of humor serves as a powerful tool, reinforcing the idea that effective leadership isn't just about making tough decisions but also about connecting, engaging, and inspiring teams in a genuine and approachable manner.

Benefits of Humor in Leadership

1. **Building Connections**: At its core, leadership is about forging meaningful connections with those you lead, and humor emerges as a potent tool in this endeavor. Shared laughter acts as a

universal language, transcending hierarchies, cultural differences, and personal boundaries. When leaders and teams share a moment of genuine amusement, it creates a bond, a shared experience that can break down formalities and foster a genuine sense of camaraderie. This mutual sense of joy and understanding can bridge gaps, making leaders more approachable and teams more cohesive. In essence, humor, when used judiciously, can transform the dynamics of a workplace, turning it from a mere place of employment to a community where individuals connect, collaborate, and thrive together.

2. **Alleviating Tension**: The corporate world, with its deadlines, challenges, and high stakes, can often be a cauldron of stress and tension. In such high-pressure environments, the strategic use of humor by leaders can act as a release valve. A well-timed joke, a playful remark, or even a light-hearted anecdote can shift the atmosphere, diffusing tension and providing a momentary respite from the weight of challenges. By introducing humor, leaders signal to their teams that while the task at hand

is essential, it's also crucial to maintain perspective and not be overwhelmed. This touch of levity can make challenges seem more manageable, providing teams with the mental space and resilience to navigate obstacles with a balanced and positive mindset.

3. **Boosting Morale**: The emotional and psychological well-being of employees plays a pivotal role in the overall health of an organization. A workplace that not only tolerates but actively embraces light-hearted moments and humor is likely to witness higher levels of employee satisfaction and morale. When leaders incorporate humor into their interactions, it creates an environment where employees feel valued, not just for their professional contributions but also for their individual personalities and quirks. This sense of belonging and validation boosts morale, leading to increased productivity, reduced turnover, and a general atmosphere of positivity and enthusiasm. In short, humor, when integrated into leadership, becomes a catalyst for creating a vibrant, motivated, and satisfied

workforce.

Potential Pitfalls and How to Avoid Them

1. **Over-reliance on Humor**: Humor, with its undeniable charm and ability to connect, can sometimes become a crutch for leaders, leading to an over-reliance on its use. While humor is a potent tool in a leader's arsenal, it's essential to remember that leadership encompasses a broad spectrum of skills and approaches. Relying solely on humor can dilute the gravity of certain situations or even undermine a leader's authority and credibility. Effective leadership requires a delicate balance of seriousness and levity, of command and camaraderie. Leaders should be wary of using humor as a default response to every situation. Instead, they should strive for a harmonious blend of humor with other leadership qualities like decisiveness, empathy, and vision. In essence, while humor can enhance leadership, it should complement, not dominate, a leader's approach.

2. **Misjudged Humor**: The subjective nature of humor means that jokes or remarks, no matter how well-intentioned, can sometimes miss the

mark or even offend. Leaders, given their position of influence, should be particularly cautious about this pitfall. What might be intended as a light-hearted jest could be perceived as insensitivity or even bias, leading to discomfort or alienation among team members. When humor is misjudged, it's crucial for leaders to promptly acknowledge the oversight, offer sincere apologies, and take it as a learning opportunity. By doing so, they not only rectify the immediate situation but also demonstrate accountability and a commitment to continuous growth and understanding.

3. **Timing**: The adage "timing is everything" holds particularly true for humor in leadership. While humor can be a valuable asset, discerning when to introduce it is equally important. There are moments that demand seriousness, empathy, or solemnity, and introducing humor in such instances can be inappropriate or even detrimental. Leaders should cultivate a keen sense of discernment, recognizing when levity can enhance a situation and when it might detract from it. This involves being attuned to the mood, context, and the emotional

undercurrents of a situation. By mastering the art of timing, leaders can ensure that their use of humor is not just effective but also respectful and appropriate to the context at hand.

In Conclusion

Humor, when used judiciously, can be a powerful tool in a leader's arsenal. It humanizes leaders, making them more relatable and approachable. In the context of the DHB Method, humor complements the principles of empathy, respect, and kindness, creating a holistic approach to leadership. As we continue our journey, we'll see how these elements interplay, crafting a leadership style that's both effective and endearing.

Chapter 5: Building Trust and Credibility

Trust is the bedrock of any successful relationship, and in the workplace, it's no different. For leaders, building and maintaining trust is paramount. It's the invisible thread that binds teams, fuels collaboration, and fosters loyalty. In the DHB Method, trust isn't just a byproduct; it's a deliberate outcome of consistent actions and behaviors. In this chapter, we'll explore the intricacies of trust, its significance in leadership, and the steps leaders can take to cultivate it.

The Anatomy of Trust

Trust is multifaceted. It's not just about believing what someone says, but also about relying on them to act in a consistent, reliable manner. Trust comprises:

- **Reliability**: At the heart of trust lies the fundamental question: Can I count on you? Reliability is the bedrock upon which trust is built. It's about consistency, about showing up, and about delivering on promises time and time again. When individuals demonstrate reliability, they signal to others that their words are not mere declarations but commitments that will be honored. Over time, as actions consistently align with words, a track record of

dependability is established. This consistency
fosters a sense of security and assurance,
allowing for deeper connections and
collaborations. In essence, reliability is the
foundation that assures others that they can
place their confidence in you, knowing that you
won't let them down.

- **Integrity**: Beyond just doing what one says,
  trust also delves into the realm of character,
  and this is where integrity comes into play.
  Integrity is about acting in a manner that's
  honest, transparent, and consistent with one's
  values, even when no one is watching. It's about
  making decisions that are not just expedient but
  also ethically sound. When individuals operate
  with integrity, they send a powerful message
  about their character, signaling that they can be
  trusted to make decisions that are in line with
  moral and ethical standards. Trust rooted in
  integrity is profound, as it assures others that
  the individual is not just reliable in action but
  also principled in intent.

- **Intent**: Trust is not just about actions; it's also
  deeply intertwined with motivations. Intent
  delves into the underlying reasons behind

actions, seeking to understand whether they are driven by genuine concern, the well-being of the team, or self-serving motives. When actions are perceived to be driven by positive and altruistic intentions, trust flourishes. It assures team members that they are valued and that decisions, even tough ones, are made with their best interests in mind. Understanding and believing in the good intent of others fosters a sense of security and loyalty, reinforcing the bonds of trust.

- **Competence**: Trust also encompasses the belief in an individual's capabilities. Competence is about having the requisite skills, knowledge, and expertise to effectively execute tasks or make informed decisions. When individuals demonstrate competence in their roles, it instills confidence in others that they are well-equipped to handle challenges and deliver on commitments. Trust based on competence is particularly crucial in professional settings, where the stakes are high, and the margin for error is slim. By consistently showcasing competence, individuals assure others that they are not just well-intentioned but also well-prepared to meet and exceed expectations.

The Importance of Trust in a Team Environment

1. **Enhanced Collaboration**: Trust acts as the lifeblood of effective collaboration in a team environment. When team members have unwavering trust in their leaders, it creates a space where open dialogue, brainstorming, and the exchange of ideas become the norm rather than the exception. This trust ensures that individuals feel valued and respected, paving the way for them to share their insights, innovations, and perspectives without the looming fear of ridicule or dismissal. It's in this atmosphere of mutual trust that the true potential of a team is unlocked. Members become more receptive to each other's viewpoints, fostering a culture of collective problem-solving and co-creation. In essence, trust transforms a group of individuals into a cohesive unit, where collaboration is not just encouraged but celebrated.

2. **Increased Productivity**: The presence of trust within a team has a direct and positive impact

on productivity. In environments where trust is prevalent, there's a marked reduction in the need for constant oversight or micromanagement. Team members, confident in the trust placed in them, are empowered to take initiative, make decisions, and execute tasks autonomously. This autonomy, rooted in trust, eliminates unnecessary bottlenecks and streamlines work processes. Moreover, when individuals know that their leaders trust them, it acts as a powerful motivator, driving them to deliver their best work consistently. The result is a team that operates efficiently, with members taking ownership of their roles and contributing proactively to the collective goals.

3. **Emotional Safety**: Trust is not just about tasks and productivity; it's deeply intertwined with the emotional well-being of team members. A trusting environment is synonymous with emotional safety, a space where employees feel secure enough to express their genuine feelings, voice concerns, or provide candid feedback. In such environments, vulnerabilities are not seen as weaknesses but as avenues for growth and understanding. When trust is

established, it assures team members that their emotions and perspectives are valued, leading to open and honest communication. This emotional safety net fosters resilience, as team members know they can navigate challenges, seek support, and express dissenting opinions without fear of retribution or alienation. In the long run, this emotional security strengthens team bonds, ensuring that members are not just working together but are genuinely invested in each other's well-being and success.

Steps to Build and Maintain Trust

1. **Consistent Communication**: In the intricate dance of trust-building, communication emerges as a pivotal step. It's not just about relaying information but doing so with clarity, timeliness, and consistency. Leaders who prioritize regular updates, ensuring their team is informed about organizational changes, pivotal decisions, and the rationale behind them, create an environment of transparency. This consistent communication eliminates the shadows of doubt and speculation, ensuring that team members are never left in the dark.

Moreover, by explaining the 'why' behind decisions, leaders offer a deeper insight into their thought processes, fostering a sense of inclusion and mutual respect. In essence, consistent communication is the bridge that connects leaders to their teams, ensuring that trust is not eroded by misinformation or ambiguity.

2. **Follow Through on Commitments**: Trust, at its core, is built on the bedrock of reliability. When leaders make promises or commitments, the onus is on them to deliver. Every fulfilled promise reinforces the perception of the leader as dependable, while every lapse can chip away at the edifice of trust. It's this consistency in honoring commitments that signals to the team that their leader's word is not just a declaration but a binding commitment. Over time, as leaders consistently follow through on their promises, it establishes a track record of dependability, assuring team members that they can place their confidence in their leader's words and actions.

3. **Admit Mistakes**: The journey of leadership, like any other, is fraught with its share of

missteps and errors. However, what differentiates a trust-inspiring leader from others is the ability to own up to these mistakes. Admitting errors is not a sign of weakness; instead, it showcases humility, accountability, and a commitment to growth. By acknowledging mistakes and taking proactive steps to rectify them, leaders send a powerful message to their teams: that they value integrity over ego and are dedicated to continuous improvement. This candidness not only bolsters trust but also creates a culture where mistakes are viewed as learning opportunities rather than failures.

4. **Seek Feedback**: Trust is a two-way street, and one of the most effective ways to fortify it is by actively seeking feedback. Leaders who invite opinions, listen to concerns, and are open to making changes based on feedback demonstrate a genuine interest in the perspectives of their team members. This act of seeking feedback is not just about gathering information; it's a testament to the leader's respect for the collective wisdom of the team. By valuing and acting upon feedback, leaders cultivate an environment of mutual respect,

where trust is continually reinforced through open dialogue and collaborative problem-solving.

5. **Be Transparent**: In the quest to build trust, transparency emerges as a cardinal virtue. Leaders who share not just the successes but also the challenges foster a sense of inclusivity and shared ownership. This openness ensures that team members are privy to the bigger picture, understanding both the triumphs and the tribulations. By being transparent, leaders eliminate the barriers of hierarchy, creating a collaborative space where everyone is informed and invested. This sense of shared reality, where both the highs and lows are communicated openly, nurtures a deep-seated trust, ensuring that the team remains united, both in times of prosperity and adversity.

The Consequences of Broken Trust and Ways to Mend It

Broken trust can have severe repercussions:

- **Reduced Morale**: Trust is the invisible glue that binds teams together, fostering a sense of unity, purpose, and mutual respect. When this trust is broken, the repercussions are felt deeply, often manifesting as a significant dip in team morale. Feelings of betrayal, disillusionment, and being undervalued can permeate the team environment. Members may start to question their worth within the organization, wondering if their contributions are genuinely valued or if they're merely cogs in a machine. This erosion of trust can lead to a pervasive sense of cynicism, where team members become disenchanted, not just with leadership but with the organization's broader vision and goals. Over time, this reduced morale can sap the enthusiasm and passion from even the most dedicated employees, turning vibrant workspaces into mere transactional environments.

- **Decreased Productivity**: Trust is a foundational element for efficient and

collaborative work. When team members trust
their leadership and each other, they can
operate with a sense of autonomy, confident
that their actions and decisions are supported.
However, when trust is compromised,
skepticism and doubt creep in. These feelings
can lead to second-guessing, hesitation, and a
reluctance to take initiatives. Collaboration,
which thrives on open communication and
mutual respect, can become stunted as team
members become wary of sharing ideas or
voicing opinions. The ripple effect of this
mistrust is a tangible decrease in productivity.
Tasks that once flowed smoothly may now be
mired in bureaucracy, hesitancy, and
miscommunication, leading to inefficiencies and
missed opportunities.

- **Increased Turnover**: One of the most telling
  indicators of broken trust is an increase in
  employee turnover. Employees, especially top
  talent, seek work environments where they feel
  valued, heard, and trusted. When trust in
  leadership is eroded, it creates a chasm
  between employees and the organization. This
  disconnect can make employees question their

long-term prospects within the company, leading them to seek opportunities elsewhere. The departure of skilled and experienced team members can have a cascading effect, not just in terms of lost expertise but also in sending a signal to remaining employees about the state of the organization. High turnover rates can further exacerbate trust issues, creating a cycle where mistrust leads to departures, which in turn fuels further mistrust. In the long run, this can have significant implications for the organization's reputation, growth, and sustainability.

Mending broken trust is challenging but not impossible:

1. **Acknowledge the Breach**: The first step towards mending broken trust is acknowledging that a breach has occurred. Denial or avoidance can exacerbate the situation, further alienating those who feel betrayed. By recognizing and accepting the lapse, leaders send a clear message that they are aware of the impact of their actions and are willing to take responsibility. This acknowledgment is not just

about admitting fault but also about understanding the depth of the emotions and disillusionment felt by the aggrieved parties. It's a crucial step that sets the tone for the subsequent healing process, demonstrating humility, accountability, and a genuine desire to set things right..

2. **Open Dialogue**: Once the breach is acknowledged, the next step is to foster open dialogue. This involves creating a safe and non-judgmental space where affected individuals can voice their feelings, concerns, and perceptions about the breach. Leaders should approach these conversations with empathy, actively listening to the concerns raised, and seeking to understand the depth of the hurt caused. This dialogue is not just about addressing the specific incident but also about uncovering any underlying issues or perceptions that might have contributed to the breach. By promoting open communication, leaders pave the way for mutual understanding, ensuring that all parties feel heard and valued.

3. **Commit to Change**: Acknowledgment and dialogue, while crucial, are just the beginning.

To truly mend broken trust, there needs to be a tangible commitment to change. This involves outlining clear steps and measures to prevent future breaches. Whether it's implementing new policies, offering training, or making structural changes, the key is to demonstrate a proactive approach to rectification. But commitment isn't just about outlining steps; it's about following through on them. Consistency in action, ensuring that promises are kept and changes are implemented, is vital. By committing to change and delivering on that commitment, leaders can start to rebuild the lost trust, demonstrating that lessons have been learned and that the organization is dedicated to growth and improvement.

4. **Rebuild Slowly**: Trust, once broken, is not something that can be restored overnight. It's a delicate fabric that needs to be woven back together with care, patience, and consistency. Leaders should recognize that trust rebuilding is a gradual process, often marked by small, consistent actions that demonstrate reliability, integrity, and genuine concern. It's essential to be patient during this phase, understanding

that trust is rebuilt one action at a time. There might be setbacks along the way, but with perseverance and a genuine commitment to restoration, it's possible to mend the bonds of trust, ensuring that they emerge stronger and more resilient than before.

In Conclusion

Trust is not a luxury in leadership; it's a necessity. In the DHB Method, trust intertwines with the pillars of empathy, respect, integrity, and kindness, creating a leadership style that's both compassionate and effective. As we delve deeper into the DHB approach, we'll see how trust acts as the foundation upon which other principles stand, ensuring a holistic and harmonious work environment.

Chapter 6: The DHB Approach to Conflict Resolution

Even in the most harmonious workplaces, conflicts are inevitable. Differences in opinions, perspectives, and approaches can lead to disagreements. However, it's not the presence of conflict that defines a team, but how it's addressed. The DHB Method offers a unique approach to conflict resolution, rooted in the principles of decency and understanding. In this chapter, we'll explore the DHB approach to resolving conflicts and fostering a culture of open dialogue and mutual respect.

Understanding the Root Causes of Workplace Conflicts

To address conflicts effectively, it's crucial to understand their root causes:

1. **Miscommunication**: One of the most common catalysts for conflicts in any setting, be it professional or personal, is miscommunication. When information is not conveyed clearly, ambiguities arise, leading to misunderstandings and, subsequently, disagreements. These misunderstandings can stem from a myriad of sources: unclear instructions, assumptions

made without verification, or even nuances lost in non-verbal communication. In today's digital age, where much of our communication happens through emails or messages, the absence of tone and body language can further exacerbate these misinterpretations. Over time, what might start as a minor miscommunication can snowball into significant disputes, especially if not addressed promptly. Addressing miscommunication requires clarity, active listening, and the willingness to seek and provide feedback to ensure all parties are on the same page.

2. **Differing Values or Goals**: In diverse teams, it's natural for individuals to bring their unique perspectives, values, and objectives to the table. While this diversity can be a strength, fostering innovation and varied viewpoints, it can also be a source of conflict if team members have differing priorities. For instance, one team member might prioritize long-term growth, while another might focus on short-term gains. These differing values or goals can lead to disagreements on strategies, resource allocation, or even the broader vision of a

project. Addressing such conflicts requires open dialogue, where team members can express their viewpoints, find common ground, and collaboratively chart a path forward that respects and integrates diverse perspectives.

3. **Resource Limitations**: Scarcity, whether in terms of time, money, or other resources, can be a significant source of tension within teams. When resources are limited, competition can arise, with team members vying for what they believe is necessary for their tasks or projects. This competition can lead to conflicts, especially if there's a perception of favoritism or inequitable distribution. Addressing conflicts arising from resource limitations requires transparent communication about the available resources, clear criteria for their allocation, and, where possible, collaborative decision-making to ensure that resources are utilized optimally and equitably.

4. **Personality Clashes**: Every individual brings their unique personality, temperament, and working style to a team. While these differences can often complement each other, there are instances where they might clash. For example,

an introverted team member might prefer detailed written communication, while an extroverted colleague might favor face-to-face discussions. Such differences, if not understood and managed, can lead to frustrations, misunderstandings, and conflicts. Addressing personality clashes requires a blend of self-awareness, empathy, and flexibility. Team members need to recognize their own preferences and be open to understanding and adapting to the styles of their colleagues. Regular team-building exercises and open discussions can also help in bridging these differences, fostering a culture of mutual respect and understanding.

The DHB Approach to Conflict Resolution

1. **Active Listening**: At the heart of the DHB approach to conflict resolution is the principle of active listening. Before formulating responses or drawing conclusions, it's imperative to genuinely listen to all parties involved in the conflict. This means not just hearing the words but understanding the underlying sentiments, concerns, and nuances.

Active listening requires setting aside biases, preconceived notions, and the urge to interject or defend. By giving each party the space and time to express themselves fully, leaders can grasp the crux of the issue, ensuring that solutions are not just surface-level but address the root of the conflict. This approach not only aids in resolving the immediate disagreement but also demonstrates respect and value for each individual's perspective.

2. **Empathy First**: Conflicts, by their very nature, are charged with emotions. The DHB approach emphasizes the importance of approaching these situations with empathy as the primary tool. Instead of entering the conflict with a combative mindset, aiming to "win" the argument, leaders should strive to understand the emotions and motivations driving each party. Recognizing and validating these emotions can defuse tensions, making it easier to navigate the conflict towards a resolution. An empathetic approach ensures that individuals feel seen and heard, laying the groundwork for constructive dialogue and collaborative problem-solving.

3. **Open Dialogue**: Beyond listening and empathy, the DHB approach champions the importance of open dialogue. This involves creating an environment where all parties involved in the conflict feel safe to express their views, concerns, and feelings without fear of retribution or judgment. Such a space promotes honest communication, allowing underlying issues to surface and be addressed. Leaders play a crucial role in facilitating this dialogue, ensuring that the conversation remains respectful, focused, and constructive. By promoting open dialogue, the DHB approach ensures that conflicts are not just resolved but also serve as learning opportunities for the team.

4. **Seek Win-Win Solutions**: Traditional conflict resolution often seeks to find a compromise, which might leave all parties somewhat dissatisfied. The DHB approach, however, aims for win-win solutions. Instead of imposing top-down decisions, leaders collaborate with the involved parties to brainstorm and identify solutions that address the needs and concerns of everyone involved. This collaborative

approach not only leads to more sustainable solutions but also fosters a sense of ownership and commitment among team members. By seeking win-win outcomes, the DHB approach ensures that conflicts become opportunities for growth and collaboration.

5. **Follow-up**: Resolving a conflict is not a one-time event but an ongoing process. The DHB approach recognizes the importance of follow-up after a resolution has been reached. Leaders should check in periodically with the involved parties to ensure that the agreed-upon solution is working effectively and to address any residual feelings or concerns. This proactive follow-up demonstrates a continued commitment to the well-being of team members and ensures that any potential issues are addressed promptly. By maintaining open channels of communication post-resolution, the DHB approach ensures that trust is rebuilt and strengthened over time.

The Role of Emotional Intelligence in Conflict Resolution

Emotional Intelligence (EI) is the ability to recognize, understand, and manage our own emotions while also recognizing, understanding, and influencing the emotions of others. In conflict resolution, EI plays a pivotal role:

- **Self-awareness**: At the foundation of Emotional Intelligence (EI) is the principle of self-awareness. This involves a deep introspection into one's own emotional landscape, especially during conflicts. Recognizing one's own emotions, triggers, and inherent biases is crucial in understanding how these factors might influence one's reactions and perceptions in a contentious situation. By being self-aware, individuals can better discern the difference between the objective facts of a conflict and their personal emotional responses to it. This clarity is invaluable, as it allows for a more grounded and objective approach to resolution, ensuring that personal biases or emotional reactions don't cloud judgment or escalate the situation.

- **Self-regulation**: Beyond recognizing one's emotions, Emotional Intelligence also emphasizes the importance of self-regulation. This is the ability to manage and control impulsive reactions, especially in emotionally charged situations. Conflicts, by their very nature, can evoke strong emotional responses, from anger to defensiveness. Self-regulation involves taking a step back, assessing these emotions, and choosing a thoughtful and measured response over a knee-jerk reaction. By doing so, individuals can prevent unnecessary escalation and ensure that the focus remains on resolving the conflict rather than intensifying it. Moreover, self-regulation fosters an environment of respect, where all parties feel that their emotions and perspectives are being considered and valued.

- **Social Awareness**: While self-awareness and self-regulation focus on one's own emotions, social awareness shifts the focus outward, emphasizing the importance of understanding the emotions and needs of others involved in the conflict. This facet of EI involves picking up on emotional cues, understanding the underlying sentiments, and recognizing the potential motivations or concerns driving the other party's stance. By being socially aware, individuals can approach conflicts with a more holistic perspective, ensuring that solutions are not just based on their own needs but also consider the emotions and needs of others. This understanding fosters empathy, making it easier to find common ground and collaborative solutions.

- **Relationship Management**: The culmination of the principles of Emotional Intelligence in conflict resolution is evident in relationship management. This involves leveraging one's understanding of both personal and social emotions to navigate interactions and steer them towards amicable resolutions. Effective relationship management ensures that conflicts, while inevitable, become opportunities for growth, understanding, and strengthened bonds. By prioritizing open communication, mutual respect, and collaborative problem-solving, individuals can ensure that conflicts are resolved in a manner that not only addresses the immediate issue but also enhances the overall health and dynamics of the relationship.

Practical Steps for Implementing the DHB Approach

1. **Training**: One of the foundational steps to effectively implementing the DHB (Decent Human Being) Approach in any organization is to provide comprehensive training sessions. These sessions should not only focus on the theoretical aspects of conflict resolution but also emphasize the unique principles and values inherent to the DHB Method. By offering such training, organizations equip their team members with the tools and knowledge they need to navigate conflicts in a constructive, empathetic, and solution-oriented manner. Moreover, these sessions can serve as platforms for team members to engage in role-playing exercises, case studies, and group discussions, allowing them to practice and internalize the DHB principles in a controlled environment. Over time, this training ensures that the DHB approach becomes an integral part of the

organization's culture, guiding interactions and decisions at all levels.

2. **Mediation**: Despite the best training and intentions, there will be instances where conflicts reach a level of complexity or intensity that requires external intervention. In such cases, the DHB approach recommends the use of mediation. By bringing in a neutral third party, organizations can ensure that the discussion remains objective, focused, and free from inherent biases or power dynamics. A skilled mediator can guide the conversation, ensuring that all parties feel heard, and help identify mutually agreeable solutions. Mediation not only aids in resolving the immediate conflict but also provides valuable insights into underlying issues or dynamics that might need addressing, ensuring long-term harmony and collaboration.

3. **Feedback Mechanisms**: An essential aspect of the DHB approach is the emphasis on open communication and the importance of listening. To foster this, organizations should establish clear and accessible feedback mechanisms. These channels allow team members to voice

their concerns, grievances, or suggestions, ensuring that they feel valued and heard. Moreover, by offering the option of anonymity, organizations can ensure that team members feel safe in sharing their feedback, free from the fear of retribution or backlash. Such feedback mechanisms are invaluable in identifying potential areas of concern, allowing leadership to address issues proactively and ensuring that the organization's culture remains aligned with the DHB principles.

4. **Regular Check-ins**: Proactive conflict resolution is at the heart of the DHB approach. Instead of waiting for issues to escalate, organizations should prioritize regular check-ins, be it through team meetings or one-on-one sessions. These check-ins serve as platforms for open dialogue, where team members can discuss their challenges, aspirations, and any potential areas of concern. By addressing issues in their nascent stages, leaders can prevent them from escalating into significant conflicts, ensuring a harmonious and collaborative work environment. Moreover, these regular interactions foster a sense of community and

trust, reinforcing the belief that the organization genuinely cares about the well-being and growth of its team members.

In Conclusion

Conflicts, while challenging, offer an opportunity for growth, understanding, and strengthening team bonds. The DHB Method's approach to conflict resolution ensures that disagreements are addressed with empathy, respect, and a genuine desire for mutual understanding. As we continue our exploration of the DHB Method, we'll see how these principles, when applied consistently, can transform not just conflicts but the very fabric of workplace interactions.

Chapter 7: Empowering and Uplifting Your Team

At the heart of the DHB Method lies a profound respect for the individual. Beyond the metrics, targets, and performance charts, there's an understanding that every team member brings unique value, potential, and aspirations. Empowering and uplifting your team isn't just about boosting productivity; it's about recognizing and nurturing the human potential within each individual. In this chapter, we'll delve into the significance of empowerment and the steps leaders can take to uplift their teams.

The Essence of Empowerment

Empowerment is more than just delegating tasks or giving autonomy. It's about:

1. **Trust**: At the heart of empowerment lies trust. It's not merely about assigning tasks or responsibilities; it's about having an unwavering belief in your team's capabilities and judgment. Trusting your team means resisting the urge to micromanage, allowing them the freedom to approach challenges in their own way, and believing that they will make decisions that

align with the organization's best interests. This trust is built over time and is based on consistent performance, open communication, and mutual respect. When team members feel trusted, they are more likely to take ownership of their roles, be proactive in problem-solving, and feel a deeper connection to their work and the organization's broader mission. In essence, trust is the foundation upon which empowerment is built, fostering an environment where individuals feel valued and confident in their contributions.

2. **Support**: Empowerment doesn't mean leaving team members to fend for themselves. It's about providing them with the necessary support to excel in their roles. This support can come in various forms, from providing the necessary resources and tools to ensuring they have access to relevant training and development opportunities. It also means being available for guidance when needed, offering insights, feedback, and mentorship. By ensuring that team members have a robust support system, organizations pave the way for them to take on challenges, innovate, and grow in their roles.

Empowerment, in this context, is about creating an environment where team members have everything they need to succeed and feel confident in seeking help or resources when they encounter obstacles.

3. **Recognition**: While trust and support are foundational to empowerment, recognition is the fuel that keeps the flame alive. Recognizing and celebrating achievements, both big and small, is crucial in reinforcing the value of each team member's contributions. It's not just about acknowledging the end results but also appreciating the effort, creativity, and resilience displayed along the way. Recognition can come in various forms, from public accolades in team meetings to personalized notes of appreciation. When team members feel seen and appreciated, their motivation, commitment, and sense of belonging to the organization soar. In essence, recognition is a powerful tool in the empowerment toolkit, ensuring that team members feel valued and inspired to continue making meaningful contributions.

Benefits of an Empowered Team

1. **Increased Motivation**: One of the most profound benefits of an empowered team is the noticeable surge in motivation levels. When team members feel that their contributions are trusted and valued, they experience a heightened sense of ownership and responsibility towards their roles and the broader organizational goals. This trust acts as a catalyst, driving them to put in their best efforts, take initiatives, and go the extra mile. They no longer see their tasks as mere assignments but as opportunities to make a meaningful impact. This intrinsic motivation, rooted in trust and empowerment, not only enhances individual performance but also contributes to a more vibrant and energized work environment, where every team member is driven by a shared sense of purpose and commitment.

2. **Enhanced Innovation**: Empowerment and innovation go hand in hand. When individuals feel empowered, they are more inclined to think outside the box, challenge the status quo, and propose novel solutions to existing problems.

The freedom to experiment, take calculated risks, and voice unconventional ideas without fear of retribution fosters a culture of creativity and continuous improvement. In such an environment, team members collaborate, share diverse perspectives, and build upon each other's ideas, leading to breakthrough solutions and advancements. Organizations that prioritize empowerment, therefore, position themselves at the forefront of innovation, continuously evolving and adapting to the ever-changing business landscape.

3. **Reduced Turnover**: Employee retention is a significant concern for many organizations, and empowerment plays a pivotal role in addressing this challenge. Employees who feel empowered in their roles experience a deeper connection to the organization, its values, and its mission. They feel that they are not just cogs in a machine but valuable contributors to the organization's success. This sense of belonging and value translates into increased loyalty and commitment. When employees believe that they have the autonomy to make decisions, the resources to perform their roles effectively, and

the recognition for their efforts, they are less likely to seek opportunities elsewhere. In essence, an empowered work environment becomes a key differentiator, making organizations more attractive to talent and reducing the costs and disruptions associated with high turnover rates.

The DHB Approach to Empowerment

1. **Decentralized Decision-Making**: The DHB (Decent Human Being) Approach places a significant emphasis on decentralized decision-making. This means moving away from a top-down, hierarchical structure where decisions are made solely at the top and trickled down. Instead, team members are encouraged to take ownership of their projects, actively participate in the decision-making process, and contribute their insights and expertise. While the ultimate accountability might still rest with the leadership, the process of arriving at decisions becomes a collaborative effort. This approach not only speeds up the decision-making process by leveraging the collective intelligence of the team but also instills a sense of responsibility and ownership among team members. They feel

more connected to the outcomes, knowing that
their input was valued and considered. In
essence, decentralized decision-making under
the DHB approach fosters a culture of trust,
collaboration, and shared responsibility.

2. **Continuous Learning**: The DHB Approach
   recognizes that for empowerment to be truly
   effective, it must be accompanied by
   opportunities for continuous learning.
   Empowerment is not just about granting
   autonomy but also ensuring that team members
   have the skills, knowledge, and resources to
   excel in their roles. Investing in training and
   development becomes paramount. Team
   members are encouraged to upskill, delve into
   new areas of expertise, and pursue avenues that
   contribute to their professional and personal
   growth. By prioritizing continuous learning,
   organizations not only enhance the capabilities
   of their teams but also demonstrate a genuine
   commitment to their growth and well-being.
   This fosters a culture where empowerment is
   not just about responsibility but also about
   growth, exploration, and continuous evolution.

3. **Open Feedback Channels**: True
   empowerment is rooted in open communication,
   and the DHB Approach underscores the
   importance of open feedback channels. In an
   empowered environment, feedback isn't a one-
   way street where leaders provide guidance and
   team members merely receive it. Instead,
   feedback becomes a dynamic exchange where
   leaders offer guidance, insights, and
   constructive criticism, while also being
   receptive to feedback about their leadership
   style, decisions, and approach. Creating such an
   environment requires trust, humility, and a
   genuine commitment to growth. When team
   members feel that their feedback is valued and
   that they can voice their opinions without fear
   of retribution, it leads to more honest,
   constructive, and actionable insights. This two-
   way feedback mechanism ensures that
   empowerment is not just about autonomy but
   also about continuous improvement,
   collaboration, and mutual respect.

Uplifting Your Team: Beyond Empowerment

Empowerment lays the foundation, but uplifting your team takes it a step further:

1. **Personalized Recognition**: While empowerment gives team members the autonomy and trust to perform their roles effectively, uplifting them requires a deeper understanding of what truly motivates each individual. Personalized recognition is about tailoring appreciation to the unique preferences and motivations of each team member. For some, a public acknowledgment in front of peers might be the most meaningful form of appreciation, while others might value a quiet word of thanks or a tangible reward. By taking the time to understand and recognize each team member in a manner that resonates with them, leaders not only validate their contributions but also strengthen their connection to the team and the organization. This personalized approach to recognition ensures that appreciation is not just a routine gesture but a genuine expression of value and gratitude.

2. **Mental and Emotional Well-being**: In today's fast-paced work environment, the importance of

mental and emotional well-being cannot be overstated. Uplifting your team goes beyond professional growth and delves into their holistic well-being. Recognizing the signs of burnout, stress, or emotional fatigue and addressing them proactively is crucial. Leaders should encourage regular breaks, promote a culture where taking time off is not frowned upon, and provide resources or support for those facing challenges. By prioritizing mental health, leaders send a clear message that they care about their team members as individuals, not just as contributors to the organization's bottom line. This fosters a work environment where individuals feel supported, understood, and valued, leading to increased loyalty, productivity, and overall well-being.

3. **Fostering a Sense of Purpose**: While empowerment provides team members with the autonomy and resources to perform their roles, uplifting them requires instilling a deeper sense of purpose. Every team member should understand how their role, no matter how big or small, fits into the broader objectives of the organization. Leaders should consistently

communicate the company's vision, mission, and goals, helping team members see the bigger picture and understand their role in achieving it. When individuals see the direct impact of their work and realize they are making a tangible difference, it instills a sense of pride, motivation, and commitment. By fostering this sense of purpose, leaders not only uplift their teams professionally but also enrich their personal sense of fulfillment and achievement.

Challenges in Empowerment and How to Overcome Them

1. **Fear of Losing Control**: One of the most common challenges leaders face when considering empowerment is the fear of losing control. This fear often stems from the misconception that empowerment equates to a complete relinquishment of authority and oversight. However, true empowerment is not about leaders giving up power but rather about distributing it in a way that allows team members to take ownership of their roles and responsibilities. By doing so, leaders are not diminishing their influence but amplifying it

through the collective efforts of an empowered team. It's essential for leaders to shift their mindset from one of control to one of trust. Empowering teams means trusting them with the autonomy to make decisions, innovate, and drive results. When leaders embrace this trust-based approach, they often find that not only do they retain control, but the outcomes often exceed their expectations due to the collective capabilities of an empowered team.

2. **Potential Mistakes**: Empowerment, by its very nature, involves granting team members the autonomy to make decisions, and with that autonomy comes the inevitable possibility of errors. However, it's crucial for organizations to foster a culture where mistakes are not seen as failures but as valuable learning opportunities. Instead of penalizing errors, leaders should encourage open discussions about them, dissecting what went wrong, and identifying lessons learned. This approach not only reduces the fear of making mistakes but also promotes a growth mindset, where continuous learning and improvement are prioritized. By reframing mistakes as stepping stones to progress, leaders

can ensure that empowerment leads to both individual and organizational growth.

3. **Resistance to Change**: Empowerment often represents a significant shift from traditional hierarchical structures, and such changes can be met with resistance from team members accustomed to clear directives and top-down decision-making. This resistance can stem from various sources, including fear of the unknown, concerns about increased responsibilities, or simply a preference for familiar routines. Overcoming this resistance requires continuous communication, where the benefits of empowerment are clearly articulated, and concerns are addressed openly. Additionally, offering training sessions can equip team members with the skills and knowledge they need to thrive in an empowered environment. Leaders should also provide consistent support during the transition, reassuring team members that while their roles might be evolving, they are not alone in the journey. Through patience, communication, and support, resistance can be transformed into acceptance and enthusiasm for the new empowered approach.

In Conclusion

Empowering and uplifting your team is the epitome of the DHB Method. It's about seeing beyond the immediate tasks and recognizing the immense potential that lies within each individual. As leaders embrace this approach, they'll find that their teams not only achieve their targets but also exceed them, driven by a sense of purpose, trust, and mutual respect. As we continue our exploration of the DHB Method, we'll see how these principles create a ripple effect, transforming the entire organizational culture.

Chapter 8: The Lighter Side of Management

In the hustle and bustle of the corporate world, it's easy to get caught up in the seriousness of it all. Deadlines, targets, and KPIs can often overshadow the human side of work. However, the DHB Method emphasizes the importance of embracing the lighter side of management. It's about finding joy in the journey, celebrating the small moments, and ensuring that work, while purposeful, also has its share of fun. In this chapter, we'll explore the significance of incorporating fun and relaxation into the workplace and its impact on productivity and team dynamics.

Why Fun Matters

1. **Stress Reduction**: In the demanding environment of the corporate world, stress is an omnipresent factor. The relentless pursuit of meeting deadlines, achieving targets, and upholding KPIs can sometimes create an atmosphere of tension and anxiety. Amidst this backdrop, the infusion of light-hearted moments becomes not just a luxury, but a necessity. These moments serve as a metaphorical release valve, allowing employees to momentarily

disconnect from the rigors of their tasks and find solace in laughter or a brief respite. By doing so, they can recalibrate, reducing the mental and emotional strain that often accompanies their roles. This isn't merely about providing a temporary escape; it's about enhancing overall well-being. When employees are given the opportunity to decompress through fun, they are better equipped to handle their responsibilities with clarity and vigor, making the workplace not just efficient, but also enjoyable.

2. **Team Bonding**: Beyond the individual, the essence of a successful corporate entity lies in its teams. The strength of a team isn't just determined by the skills or expertise it possesses, but by the bonds that tie its members together. Shared moments of fun and laughter are more than just ephemeral instances of joy; they are the threads that weave the fabric of a cohesive team. Whether it's a shared joke during a coffee break, a team outing, or simply a light-hearted chat amidst a busy day, these moments create shared memories. They bridge gaps, dissolve

hierarchies, and foster a sense of belonging. Over time, these shared experiences cultivate a deep sense of camaraderie, ensuring that team members not only work together but also genuinely care for and support one another. In the grand tapestry of corporate success, these bonds, often forged in moments of fun, play an indispensable role.

3. **Creativity Boost**: The corporate world, while structured, thrives on innovation. Every challenge, every project often requires a touch of creativity to find optimal solutions. However, creativity is not a faucet that can be turned on at will; it requires the right environment to flourish. A mind bogged down by stress and pressure is less likely to think innovatively. On the other hand, a relaxed and joyful mind, one that has experienced moments of fun and levity, is more receptive to creative thought. Such a mind is free to wander, explore, and connect dots in unconventional ways. By fostering an environment that values and promotes fun, organizations inadvertently create a hotbed for creative thinking. Employees, when relaxed and happy, are more likely to approach challenges

with a fresh perspective, brainstorm collaboratively, and come up with innovative solutions that drive success. In essence, fun becomes the catalyst that fuels the creative engine of the corporate world.

The DHB Approach to Fun at Work

1. **Regular Team-Building Activities**: In the structured environment of the corporate world, interactions often revolve around meetings, projects, and deadlines. While these are essential, they can sometimes limit the depth of relationships among team members. The DHB approach emphasizes the importance of fostering connections beyond the confines of work-related tasks. By organizing regular team-building activities, leaders can create opportunities for team members to interact in more relaxed, non-work settings. These activities, ranging from casual team lunches to more elaborate off-site retreats, allow individuals to see different facets of their colleagues, breaking down formal barriers and facilitating genuine connections. Over time, these interactions not only enhance team

cohesion but also contribute to a more harmonious and collaborative work environment.

2. **Celebrate Milestones**: In the race to achieve goals and meet targets, it's easy to overlook the journey's milestones. However, the DHB approach recognizes the significance of pausing and celebrating these moments. Whether it's the successful completion of a challenging project, a team member's birthday, or the company's anniversary, each milestone offers an opportunity to acknowledge efforts, appreciate achievements, and foster a sense of belonging. Celebrating these moments infuses positivity into the workplace, reminding everyone of their collective achievements and the shared journey. It's not just about the celebration itself but about reinforcing the message that every effort, big or small, is valued and appreciated.

3. **Encourage Breaks**: The modern work culture, with its emphasis on productivity, often pushes individuals to their limits. While dedication is commendable, non-stop work can lead to burnout and reduced efficiency. The DHB

approach champions the idea of balance. By promoting the concept of taking short, regular breaks during the day, leaders send a clear message about the importance of well-being. These breaks, whether they involve a brief walk, a quick game, or just some quiet downtime, serve as mini-refreshers, allowing individuals to reset and rejuvenate. Over time, these moments of respite can enhance overall productivity, reduce stress, and contribute to a more balanced and happy work environment.

4. **Create Fun Spaces**: Physical spaces play a pivotal role in shaping behaviors and mindsets. While traditional office setups focus on workstations and meeting rooms, the DHB approach advocates for the inclusion of dedicated fun and relaxation areas. These spaces, be it a cozy lounge, an engaging games room, or a serene reading corner, offer employees a place to disconnect from their tasks momentarily. They provide an environment where individuals can relax, engage in activities they enjoy, or simply take a moment for themselves. By creating such spaces, organizations not only cater to the well-

being of their employees but also foster a culture that values balance, fun, and holistic development.

Balancing Work and Play

While promoting fun is essential, it's equally crucial to strike a balance:

1. **Set Clear Boundaries**: The infusion of fun into the workplace is a refreshing change from traditional corporate environments. However, it's essential to remember that the primary purpose of the workplace is professional output. While fostering a relaxed atmosphere, leaders must ensure that there are clear boundaries in place. These boundaries help in distinguishing between moments of relaxation and times of focused work. By setting and communicating these limits, organizations can enjoy the benefits of a relaxed environment without compromising on the core values of professionalism and responsibility. It's about creating a harmonious blend where employees feel at ease but are also aware of when it's time to switch gears and dive into their tasks with dedication.

2. **Respect Individual Preferences**: The beauty of humanity lies in its diversity, and this extends to our preferences for relaxation and fun. In a diverse workplace, it's inevitable that everyone's idea of fun will differ. While some might find solace in a quiet reading nook, others might prefer the camaraderie of a team game. As organizations promote fun, it's crucial to be mindful of these individual preferences. Leaders should ensure that the avenues for relaxation cater to a broad spectrum of interests and that no one feels pressured to participate in activities they don't enjoy. Moreover, it's essential to ensure that the fun activities don't become a source of distraction or annoyance for those who prefer a different kind of relaxation. By respecting individual preferences, organizations can create an inclusive environment where everyone feels valued and understood.

3. **Monitor Productivity**: The ultimate goal of introducing fun into the workplace is to enhance overall well-being, which, in turn, boosts productivity. However, like all good things, it's possible to have too much of a good

thing. As organizations embrace a more relaxed atmosphere, it's vital to keep a close eye on productivity levels. Leaders should regularly assess whether the fun initiatives are complementing the work processes or hindering them. If productivity starts to dip, it might be time to reassess and recalibrate. The key is to strike a balance where employees feel rejuvenated by the fun activities, leading to increased efficiency and creativity in their tasks. It's about ensuring that relaxation serves as a catalyst for productivity, not an impediment.

Challenges and How to Address Them

1. **Misunderstandings**: The introduction of fun into the workplace can be a double-edged sword. While many will welcome the shift from a traditional corporate environment, there's a potential for misunderstandings. Some team members might interpret the newfound emphasis on relaxation and enjoyment as a sign that the organization is no longer serious about its core objectives. Such misconceptions can lead to a lack of motivation or commitment to

tasks. To address this, continuous communication is paramount. Leaders should regularly articulate the rationale behind the fun initiatives, emphasizing that the goal is to enhance well-being and productivity, not to diminish the importance of work. By consistently communicating the objectives and benefits of a balanced work environment, organizations can ensure that the team remains aligned with the company's vision and values.

2. **Overindulgence**: Every good initiative comes with its set of challenges, and the promotion of fun in the workplace is no exception. There's a tangible risk that some individuals might overindulge in the recreational activities, leading to disruptions or decreased productivity. It's essential for leaders to set clear guidelines and expectations from the outset. While the organization encourages relaxation and enjoyment, there should be a clear understanding that work responsibilities remain paramount. Periodic reviews and feedback sessions can help monitor the situation and ensure that the balance between work and play is maintained. If issues arise,

leaders should address them promptly, reinforcing the importance of balance and the primary purpose of the workplace.

3. **Diversity in Preferences**: A diverse team brings a plethora of benefits, from varied perspectives to a rich tapestry of skills. However, this diversity also means a wide range of preferences when it comes to relaxation and fun. While some might relish a team-building outdoor activity, others might prefer a quiet indoor game or even solitary relaxation. Catering to these diverse tastes can be challenging. To address this, organizations can rotate activities, ensuring that over time, every team member finds something they enjoy. Alternatively, offering multiple options simultaneously allows individuals to choose the activity that resonates most with them. By being inclusive and considerate of individual preferences, organizations can ensure that the fun initiatives are effective and appreciated by all.

In Conclusion

The DHB Method's emphasis on the lighter side of management is a testament to its holistic approach. It recognizes that while work is essential, so is well-being, joy, and relaxation. By incorporating fun into the workplace, leaders can ensure that their teams are not only productive but also happy, motivated, and engaged. As we delve deeper into the DHB Method, we'll see how this balance between work and play plays a pivotal role in shaping a positive, vibrant, and dynamic workplace culture.

Chapter 9: Real-life Success Stories

The DHB Method, while rooted in timeless principles, is more than just a theoretical approach to management. Across the globe, numerous organizations and leaders have embraced the tenets of the DHB Method, witnessing transformative results. In this chapter, we'll explore some real-life success stories that highlight the tangible benefits of leading with decency, empathy, and respect.

Company A: Embracing Empathy in Tech

In the dynamic and relentless realm of technology, where innovation is the name of the game and deadlines are ever-looming, Company A, a vanguard in the software industry, found itself grappling with a pressing issue. The rapid pace, while exhilarating, began to take a toll on its most valuable asset: its employees. The symptoms were clear - heightened levels of burnout, a palpable sense of fatigue, and an alarming rate of turnover. The company's leadership realized that to maintain its industry-leading position, a change in approach was imperative.

- **Initiatives**: Recognizing the challenges, Company A took decisive steps to infuse empathy and understanding into its work culture, drawing inspiration from the DHB Method. The company introduced flexible work hours, acknowledging that a one-size-fits-all approach to scheduling might not cater to the diverse needs of its workforce. Recognizing the mental toll that the tech industry can exert, they also championed the cause of mental well-being by offering mental health days. These days allowed employees to take a step back, rejuvenate, and return to work with renewed vigor. Beyond these measures, Company A also recognized the importance of team cohesion and camaraderie. They began organizing regular team-building retreats, providing a space for employees to connect, not just as colleagues, but as individuals. These retreats served as a melting pot of ideas, fostering innovation while also strengthening interpersonal bonds.

- **Results**: The impact of these initiatives was both immediate and profound. Company A witnessed a staggering 40% reduction in employee turnover. But the benefits weren't just in numbers. The office atmosphere underwent a transformation. There was a palpable boost in team morale, with employees feeling more valued and understood. This renewed sense of belonging and appreciation translated directly into their work, leading to a surge in innovative ideas and collaborative projects. The company's forward-thinking approach not only helped retain talent but also ensured that this talent was operating at its peak potential.

Company B: Prioritizing People in Manufacturing

In the intricate tapestry of the manufacturing sector, where precision, efficiency, and timelines are paramount, Company B stood out as a colossus. However, beneath the sheen of its massive production lines and sprawling facilities, there was a growing undercurrent of discontent. Labor disputes became frequent, echoing the sentiments of a workforce that felt undervalued and unheard. Worker satisfaction plummeted, and the ripples of this dissatisfaction began affecting production timelines and overall efficiency. The leadership of Company B, in a moment of introspection, realized that the heart of a manufacturing unit wasn't its machinery, but its people. To address these challenges, they turned to the principles of the DHB Method.

- **Initiatives**: Embracing the ethos of the DHB approach, Company B embarked on a transformative journey to prioritize its people. They introduced open feedback forums, a platform where every worker, irrespective of their position, could voice their concerns, suggestions, and feedback. These forums became a beacon of open communication, bridging the gap between the management and the shop floor. Recognizing the importance of representation, worker-led committees were established. These committees played a pivotal role in decision-making processes, ensuring that the workers' perspectives were always considered. But perhaps the most significant change was the introduction of transparent wage structures. By demystifying wages and ensuring fairness in compensation, Company B sent a clear message: every worker's contribution was recognized and valued.

- **Results**: The transformation was nothing short of remarkable. Labor disputes, which once seemed like an insurmountable challenge, decreased by a whopping 70%. But the numbers only tell a part of the story. The factory floors, once rife with tension, now buzzed with a renewed sense of purpose and collaboration. Production efficiency saw marked improvements, with projects being completed ahead of schedules and quality benchmarks consistently met. Most importantly, worker satisfaction soared. Employees now felt a sense of belonging and pride in their roles, knowing that they were an integral part of Company B's success story. The company's shift from a purely production-centric approach to one that prioritized its people became a testament to the power of the DHB Method in action.

Company C: Retail Revolution with Respect

In the bustling world of retail, where every customer interaction can make or break a brand's reputation, Company C found itself at a crossroads. As a prominent retail chain with outlets spanning multiple cities, it was disheartening for them to witness dwindling customer satisfaction rates. Concurrently, there was a palpable sense of disengagement among their employees. The vibrant energy that once characterized their stores seemed to be ebbing away. Recognizing the symbiotic relationship between employee morale and customer satisfaction, Company C's leadership decided to pivot towards a more human-centric approach, drawing inspiration from the DHB Method.

- **Initiatives**: The first order of business was to address the interaction between employees and customers. Company C rolled out comprehensive training programs that emphasized the art of active listening. Employees were trained not just to hear but to genuinely listen to customers, understanding their needs, preferences, and concerns. Alongside this, another focal point of the training was cultivating customer empathy. Employees were encouraged to put themselves in the customers' shoes, understanding their journey and ensuring that every interaction was tailored to provide a memorable shopping experience. But Company C's transformation wasn't limited to customer interactions. Recognizing the pivotal role their employees played, they introduced robust employee

recognition programs. These programs
celebrated the achievements, both big and
small, of their staff, ensuring that their
dedication and hard work never went
unnoticed.

- **Results**: The metamorphosis of Company C's
  retail outlets was evident. Customer satisfaction
  scores, which once languished, saw a robust
  30% increase. Customers began to resonate
  with the brand's renewed commitment to
  service, often lauding the attentive and
  empathetic staff. But beyond the numbers, the
  stores themselves underwent a transformation.
  The once-muted energy was replaced with a
  vibrant dynamism, with employees actively
  engaging with customers and taking pride in
  their roles. Employee engagement levels
  skyrocketed, with many reporting a renewed
  sense of purpose and enthusiasm. Company C's
  journey from facing challenges to redefining
  retail with respect showcased the
  transformative potential of the DHB Method.

Company D: Healthcare with a Heart

The healthcare sector, more than any other, hinges on the delicate balance of technical proficiency and human touch. For Company D, a sprawling network of hospitals, this balance became the focal point of their mission. While their facilities boasted state-of-the-art equipment and top-tier medical professionals, they recognized a growing need to enhance the human aspect of patient care. Simultaneously, there was an increasing concern about the well-being of their staff, who often worked long hours in high-pressure environments. The leadership of Company D realized that to truly stand out and make a difference, they needed to infuse the principles of the DHB Method into their healthcare approach.

- **Initiatives**: At the heart of Company D's transformation was the patient. Recognizing that patients were not just cases but individuals with emotions, fears, and hopes, the hospital introduced structured patient feedback sessions. These sessions provided patients with a platform to voice their experiences, concerns, and suggestions. This direct line of communication ensured that the hospital could continually refine its approach to patient care. But the changes weren't limited to patient interactions. Company D invested heavily in continuous training for its staff, focusing on enhancing their communication skills and fostering empathy. These training sessions equipped the staff to better understand and cater to the emotional and psychological needs of patients. Beyond patient care, the well-being of the staff became a priority. Regular well-being check-ins were instituted, ensuring that staff members had the necessary support, both emotionally and professionally.

- **Results**: The ripple effects of Company D's initiatives were profound. Patient recovery rates, a critical metric in healthcare, saw marked improvement. This wasn't just due to medical interventions but also because of the positive, supportive environment that patients found themselves in. On the staff front, burnout rates, which had been a growing concern, began to decrease. The regular check-ins and support mechanisms ensured that staff felt valued and cared for, translating to better patient care. But perhaps the most telling result was the reputation Company D began to garner. In a sector often criticized for its impersonal approach, Company D's network of hospitals became synonymous with compassionate care. Patients and their families began to choose Company D not just for its medical expertise but for its heart.

Challenges Faced During Transition

While the results were transformative, the journey wasn't without challenges:

1. **Initial Resistance**: Across the spectrum, from the tech-driven environment of Company A to the patient-centric world of Company D, one challenge was universal: the skepticism of long-standing employees. These individuals, having spent years, if not decades, in their respective industries, had grown accustomed to a certain way of doing things. Traditional management styles, with their clear hierarchies and task-driven focus, were familiar and comfortable. The introduction of the DHB Method, with its emphasis on empathy, empowerment, and holistic well-being, was seen by many as a radical departure from the norm. Questions arose: "Is this just a passing trend?" "How does this fit into our industry?" Overcoming this

resistance required a combination of open dialogue, patience, and demonstrable evidence that the DHB Method wasn't just a theoretical concept but had tangible benefits.

2. **Balancing Profit and People**: Each of the four companies, despite their varied sectors, grappled with a common dilemma: how to reconcile business objectives with the people-centric principles of the DHB Method. Company B, in the manufacturing sector, had to consider production targets alongside worker satisfaction. Company C, in retail, had to balance sales goals with employee engagement and customer satisfaction. The challenge was to demonstrate that these objectives weren't mutually exclusive. By prioritizing people, companies could, in fact, drive profitability. It required a shift in perspective, seeing employees not as mere resources but as invaluable assets whose well-being directly impacted the bottom line. This balance, while delicate, was achievable with strategic planning and a commitment to the DHB principles.

3. **Continuous Training**: The introduction of the DHB Method wasn't a one-time event. It was a

cultural shift, and for it to be truly effective, it required continuous reinforcement. This was a challenge that all four companies faced. Whether it was Company A, with its tech-savvy workforce, or Company D, with its healthcare professionals, the need for ongoing training was paramount. But training wasn't just about imparting skills; it was about instilling a mindset. It was about ensuring that the principles of the DHB Method became second nature to every employee, from the boardroom to the shop floor. This demanded resources, both in terms of time and finances. But the companies recognized its importance. They understood that for real transformation to occur, the principles of the DHB Method had to be ingrained in every aspect of the organization.

In Conclusion

The success stories of these companies underscore the universal applicability and tangible benefits of the DHB Method. Whether in tech, manufacturing, retail, or healthcare, leading with decency, respect, and empathy yields positive results. These stories serve as inspiration, showcasing that with commitment, understanding, and genuine care, organizations can create environments where both people and profits thrive. As we continue our exploration of the DHB Method, these real-world examples will serve as benchmarks and guiding lights.

Chapter 10: Implementing the DHB Method: A Step-by-Step Guide

Having delved deep into the principles, benefits, and real-world applications of the DHB Method, it's time to address the practical aspect: How can you, as a leader or organization, implement the DHB Method in your own workspace? This chapter provides a step-by-step guide to seamlessly integrate the principles of the DHB Method into your leadership style and organizational culture.

Step 1: Self-Assessment and Reflection

Every journey begins with understanding one's starting point. Before diving into the DHB Method, leaders must first introspect and evaluate their current leadership style. This involves taking structured leadership assessments, which can provide insights into one's strengths and potential areas for growth. But beyond formal assessments, genuine feedback from peers and subordinates can be invaluable. By actively seeking out this feedback and reflecting upon it, leaders can gain a holistic understanding of their leadership impact and identify specific areas where the DHB Method can make a difference.

- **Objective**: Understand your current leadership style and identify areas of improvement.

- **Action**: Take leadership assessments, seek feedback from peers and subordinates, and reflect on your strengths and areas of growth.

Step 2: Setting Clear Intentions

With a clear understanding of the current scenario, the next step is to define the desired outcomes. What does success look like? Whether it's fostering a more collaborative team environment, reducing employee turnover, or simply enhancing overall team morale, having clear, tangible goals provides direction and purpose to the implementation process. These intentions act as a guiding light, ensuring that every subsequent action aligns with the overarching objectives.

- **Objective**: Define what you aim to achieve by implementing the DHB Method.

- **Action**: Set clear goals, such as improving team morale, reducing turnover, or enhancing collaboration.

Step 3: Communication and Buy-in

Change, no matter how positive, can often be met with resistance or skepticism. This is why transparent communication is paramount. Leaders should proactively introduce the DHB Method to their teams, elucidating its principles and the rationale behind its adoption. Workshops, seminars, or even informal team meetings can serve as platforms for this. Addressing concerns, answering questions, and highlighting the tangible benefits of the DHB Method can ensure that the entire team is on board and invested in the journey ahead.

- **Objective**: Ensure that the team understands and supports the shift towards the DHB Method.

- **Action**: Hold team meetings, workshops, or seminars to introduce the DHB principles. Highlight the benefits and address any concerns.

Step 4: Training and Development

Understanding a concept and putting it into practice are two different things. To truly embrace the DHB Method, both leaders and team members might need to acquire or hone certain skills. This could range from active listening techniques to conflict resolution strategies. Organizing dedicated training sessions can equip the team with the necessary tools and knowledge to effectively implement the DHB principles in their daily interactions and decision-making processes.

- **Objective**: Equip yourself and your team with the skills needed to embrace the DHB Method.

- **Action**: Organize training sessions on active listening, empathy, conflict resolution, and other relevant topics.

Step 5: Policy Re-evaluation

For the DHB Method to be truly effective, it shouldn't just be an abstract concept but should be reflected in the very fabric of the organization's policies. This might involve revisiting HR policies, feedback mechanisms, and other organizational processes to ensure they align with the values of decency, respect, and empathy. Such alignment ensures that the DHB Method is not just a leadership style but becomes an integral part of the organization's ethos.

- **Objective**: Ensure that organizational policies align with the DHB principles.

- **Action**: Review and modify HR policies, feedback mechanisms, and other processes to reflect the values of decency, respect, and empathy.

Step 6: Celebrate Small Wins

Change is often a gradual process, and along the way, there will be milestones, both big and small. Recognizing and celebrating these milestones can serve as motivation, reinforcing the positive impact of the DHB Method. Whether it's a team member who exemplified empathy in a challenging situation or a notable improvement in team collaboration, these moments of success deserve acknowledgment.

- **Objective**: Recognize and reward the positive changes and milestones achieved.

- **Action**: Celebrate instances where team members exemplify the DHB principles, whether it's through public recognition, awards, or other incentives.

Step 7: Continuous Feedback and Iteration

The DHB Method is not a static model; it's dynamic and should evolve based on feedback and changing circumstances. Regularly seeking feedback from team members can provide insights into what's working and where adjustments might be needed. This iterative approach ensures that the DHB Method remains relevant and effective in addressing the unique challenges and needs of the organization.

- **Objective**: Ensure that the implementation of the DHB Method remains effective and relevant.

- **Action**: Regularly seek feedback from the team, assess the impact of changes made, and make necessary adjustments.

Step 8: Lead by Example

Perhaps the most crucial aspect of implementing the DHB Method is for leaders to embody its principles in every action and decision. When leaders consistently demonstrate decency, respect, and empathy, it sets a precedent for the entire team. It sends a clear message about what is valued and expected, creating a ripple effect throughout the organization.

- **Objective**: Be the embodiment of the DHB Method.

- **Action**: Consistently demonstrate the principles of decency, respect, and empathy in your actions, decisions, and interactions.

Step 9: Foster a Culture of Continuous Learning

For the DHB Method to have a lasting impact, it should be ingrained in the organization's culture. This involves fostering a mindset of continuous learning. Encouraging team members to attend workshops, delve into relevant literature, or engage in meaningful discussions about the DHB principles can ensure that these values remain at the forefront of the organization's ethos.

- **Objective**: Ensure that the DHB principles are ingrained in the organizational culture.

- **Action**: Encourage team members to attend workshops, read relevant literature, and engage in discussions about the DHB Method.

Step 10: Periodic Review

Lastly, it's essential to periodically assess the impact of the DHB Method. This involves measuring the actual outcomes against the initially set intentions. Whether it's through surveys, feedback sessions, or quantitative metrics, these reviews can provide valuable insights into the effectiveness of the DHB Method and highlight areas for further refinement.

- **Objective**: Assess the long-term impact and effectiveness of the DHB Method.

- **Action**: Conduct annual or bi-annual reviews to measure the outcomes against the set intentions and make necessary refinements.

In Conclusion

Implementing the DHB Method is not a one-time event but a continuous journey of growth, learning, and refinement. It requires commitment, patience, and a genuine desire to see people thrive. As you embark on this transformative journey, remember that the essence of the DHB Method lies not just in its principles but in its daily practice. With dedication and persistence, you can create a workspace where decency, respect, and empathy are not just buzzwords but a lived reality.

Chapter 11: The Future of the DHB Method

As we near the end of our exploration into the DHB Method, it's essential to look ahead. In a rapidly evolving world, with technological advancements, shifting workplace dynamics, and a renewed emphasis on mental well-being, where does the DHB Method fit in? In this chapter, we'll forecast the future trajectory of the DHB Method and its relevance in the ever-changing landscape of leadership and management.

The Rise of Remote Work

With the increasing acceptance of remote work:

- **DHB in Digital Communication** In today's digital age, where face-to-face interactions are often replaced by screens and keyboards, the essence of the DHB Method becomes even more paramount. Digital communication, while efficient, can sometimes lack the nuances and emotional cues of in-person conversations. This makes it easy for messages to be misconstrued or for sentiments to be lost in translation. By integrating the principles of the DHB Method into digital communication, leaders and teams can ensure that their interactions remain clear, respectful, and empathetic. This involves being more deliberate in crafting messages, using tools that facilitate better understanding, and always approaching digital interactions with a mindset of decency and respect.

- **Building Trust Virtually**: The traditional methods of building trust, often rooted in face-to-face interactions, shared experiences, and physical presence, face challenges in a remote work setting. In a virtual environment, leaders don't have the luxury of spontaneous hallway conversations or team lunches to foster relationships. However, the principles of the DHB Method provide a roadmap for building trust even when miles apart. It's about consistently demonstrating reliability, showing genuine concern for team members, and creating spaces for open and honest virtual conversations. Regular check-ins, transparent communication, and recognizing efforts in virtual settings can go a long way in ensuring that trust is not only established but also nurtured and maintained in remote teams.

The Emphasis on Mental Well-being

As organizations recognize the importance of mental health:

- **DHB as a Pillar of Support**: In an era where the significance of mental well-being is gaining unprecedented attention, the DHB Method emerges as a beacon of support for organizations worldwide. The principles of decency, respect, and empathy inherently align with the needs of individuals seeking understanding and support in their professional environments. By embracing the DHB Method, leaders can ensure that they're not just addressing work-related tasks but also the holistic well-being of their team members. This approach goes beyond mere task management; it delves into the realm of human connection, understanding individual struggles, and offering support. When employees feel that their leaders genuinely care about their mental health, it fosters a sense of belonging and security, making the workplace a sanctuary of support and understanding.

- **Creating Safe Spaces**: The importance of a safe space, where employees can freely express their feelings, concerns, and challenges without fear of judgment or retribution, cannot be overstated. The DHB Method provides a blueprint for leaders to create such environments. By prioritizing respect and empathy, leaders can cultivate a culture where open conversations about mental health are not just accepted but encouraged. Such spaces aren't limited to formal counseling sessions; they can be integrated into daily interactions, team meetings, and feedback sessions. When employees know that they have a platform to voice their challenges and that they will be met with understanding and support, it can significantly enhance their mental well-being and overall job satisfaction.

The Age of Automation and AI

With the rise of automation and AI:

- **DHB in Human-AI Collaboration**: In the rapidly evolving landscape of automation and artificial intelligence (AI), the DHB Method serves as a compass, guiding leaders towards a harmonious integration of technology and humanity. While AI offers unparalleled efficiency and capabilities, it's imperative that its deployment aligns with the principles of decency and humanity. This means that AI should be designed and utilized in a manner that complements human roles, rather than replacing or undermining them. Leaders, by adhering to the DHB Method, can ensure that AI systems are developed and implemented with a deep respect for human values, ethics, and rights. This approach ensures that technology acts as an enabler, enhancing the human experience, rather than creating a divide. It's about harnessing the power of AI while staying rooted in the core values that make us inherently human.

- **Valuing Human Skills**: The advent of automation and AI has undeniably transformed the job market, with many repetitive tasks now being handled by machines. However, this shift brings to the forefront the irreplaceable value of inherently human skills. The DHB Method emphasizes the significance of qualities like empathy, creativity, and collaboration—skills that machines cannot replicate. As automation takes over routine tasks, the human workforce will find its strengths in areas that require emotional intelligence, innovative thinking, and interpersonal interactions. Leaders who champion the DHB Method will be at the forefront of this transition, recognizing and nurturing these human-centric skills within their teams. By doing so, they not only prepare their organizations for a future dominated by AI but also underscore the timeless value of human touch in an increasingly automated world.

The Multigenerational Workplace

As Baby Boomers, Gen X, Millennials, and Gen Z converge in the workplace:

- **DHB Bridging Gaps**: In today's dynamic workplace, where multiple generations coexist, the potential for misunderstandings and misalignments is heightened. Each generation comes with its own set of values, experiences, and perspectives, which can sometimes lead to friction. However, the DHB Method emerges as a beacon of unity in this diverse setting. By emphasizing decency, respect, and empathy, the DHB approach ensures that every individual, irrespective of their generational background, feels valued and understood. It promotes a culture where Baby Boomers, Gen X, Millennials, and Gen Z can cohesively work together, leveraging the strengths and insights each brings to the table. By fostering an environment of mutual respect and understanding, the DHB Method bridges generational divides, creating a harmonious and productive workplace where every voice is heard and appreciated.

- **Tailored Approaches**: While the DHB Method provides a foundational approach to leadership, it also recognizes the importance of adaptability. With multiple generations in the workplace, a one-size-fits-all leadership style is unlikely to be effective. Each generation has its own aspirations, motivations, and challenges. Leaders who embrace the DHB principles are better equipped to tailor their leadership styles to cater to these unique needs. For instance, while Baby Boomers might value job security and face-to-face interactions, Millennials might prioritize work-life balance and digital communication. By understanding these nuances and adapting accordingly, leaders can ensure that they're providing the right kind of support and guidance to each generation. This tailored approach, rooted in the principles of decency, respect, and empathy, ensures that every team member feels seen, understood, and empowered, regardless of their generational background.

The Globalized Work Environment

With teams spread across continents and cultures:

- **DHB in Cultural Sensitivity**: In an era where teams are dispersed across continents, the complexities of leading become multifaceted. The globalized work environment brings together a rich tapestry of cultures, traditions, and perspectives. While this diversity is a strength, it also presents challenges in ensuring harmonious collaboration. Here, the DHB Method, with its emphasis on respect and understanding, becomes instrumental. Leaders who adopt the DHB principles are better equipped to navigate the intricate maze of cultural nuances. They approach differences not as barriers but as opportunities for learning and growth. By actively seeking to understand the cultural backgrounds of their team members, they ensure that every individual feels respected and valued. This cultural sensitivity, rooted in the DHB Method, fosters an environment where diversity is celebrated, and misunderstandings stemming from cultural differences are minimized.

- **Unified Organizational Culture**: While acknowledging and respecting cultural differences is crucial, there's also a need for a cohesive organizational culture that binds everyone together. The DHB Method plays a pivotal role in achieving this balance. It provides a framework that promotes shared values of decency, respect, and empathy, transcending geographical and cultural boundaries. Leaders who implement the DHB approach work towards creating a unified organizational culture where, despite the diverse backgrounds, everyone subscribes to a common ethos. This doesn't mean erasing individual cultural identities but rather creating an overarching culture where shared values coexist with individual cultural traits. Such a culture ensures that while employees across the globe might have different ways of celebrating festivals or communicating, they all align on the core principles of respect, understanding, and collaboration, making the organization truly global in its approach and ethos.

In Conclusion

The future of the DHB Method is not just promising; it's essential. As the world evolves, the timeless principles of decency, respect, and empathy will remain constant, guiding leaders in navigating the challenges and opportunities of the future. The DHB Method, while rooted in age-old values, is incredibly forward-looking, ensuring that leaders are equipped to lead with both competence and compassion in the decades to come. As we conclude our exploration, let the DHB Method not just be a concept you've learned but a philosophy you live by, shaping a brighter, kinder, and more inclusive future for all.

Summing Up

As we close this exploration into the DHB Method, it's essential to reflect on the journey we've undertaken. From understanding the core principles of being a Decent Human Being in leadership to diving deep into its practical applications, we've seen how transformative and impactful this approach can be. The corporate world often paints a picture of leadership as a realm of tough decisions, strategic maneuvers, and bottom-line results. While these elements are undeniably crucial, the DHB Method reminds us that at the core of every organization, team, and project are people. People with dreams, aspirations, fears, and emotions. And to lead these individuals effectively, one must lead with empathy, respect, and, above all, decency.

In a rapidly changing world, where technology, globalization, and societal shifts continually redefine the rules of the game, the DHB Method stands as a beacon of constancy. It reminds us that while strategies might change, values remain. It emphasizes that in the intricate dance of leadership, the steps might evolve, but the heart and soul—the essence of being a decent human—must remain unwavering.

For those who've journeyed through these pages, the hope is that the DHB Method becomes more than just a management style. Let it be a way of life. Let it influence not just your professional decisions but also your daily interactions. Let the principles of decency, respect, and empathy permeate every facet of your existence.

In the end, leadership, in its truest form, is not about power, control, or accolades. It's about impact. It's about making a difference in the lives of those you lead. And what better way to make a difference than by being a beacon of kindness, understanding, and humanity?

Thank you for embarking on this journey into the heart of leadership. May the DHB Method inspire, guide, and uplift you as you forge ahead, shaping a world where business thrives alongside compassion, where productivity meets empathy, and where every leader, at their core, is a Decent Human Being.

Appendix: Tools, Resources, and Further Reading

In our exploration of the DHB Method, we've touched upon various principles, techniques, and strategies. This appendix serves as a consolidated resource guide, offering tools, references, and suggestions for further reading to deepen your understanding and application of the DHB Method.

A. Tools for Implementing the DHB Method

1. **Active Listening Checklist**: A step-by-step guide to ensure you're fully present and engaged in conversations.

2. **Feedback Framework**: A structured approach to giving and receiving feedback, emphasizing clarity, kindness, and constructiveness.

3. **Conflict Resolution Flowchart**: A visual guide to navigating conflicts using the DHB principles.

4. **Empowerment Audit**: A set of questions to assess how empowered your team feels and identify areas for improvement.

B. Recommended Workshops and Training Programs

1. **"Empathy in Leadership"**: A workshop focusing on understanding and practicing empathy in everyday leadership scenarios.

2. **"Effective Communication for Modern Leaders"**: A program that combines traditional communication strategies with modern tools and platforms.

3. **"DHB Team Building Retreats"**: Tailored retreats focusing on team bonding, communication, and the principles of the DHB Method.

C. Further Reading

1. **"The Power of Vulnerability"** by Brené Brown: A deep dive into the strength that comes from embracing vulnerability, authenticity, and empathy.

2. **"Leaders Eat Last"** by Simon Sinek: An exploration of how leaders can create a culture of trust and cooperation.

3. **"Dare to Lead"** by Brené Brown: A guide to brave leadership, emphasizing the importance of courage and connection.

4. **"How to Win Friends and Influence People"** by Dale Carnegie: A timeless classic on the art of effective communication and relationship-building.

D. Acknowledgments

A special thanks to all the organizations and leaders who shared their success stories and challenges, providing invaluable insights into the real-world application of the DHB Method. Your experiences have enriched this exploration, making it both practical and relatable.

We hope this appendix serves as a handy reference as you embark on your journey with the DHB Method. Remember, the journey of leadership is one of continuous learning, growth, and reflection. May these resources guide, inspire, and support you every step of the way.